The Life and Times of
LAUREL
AND
HARDY

The Life and Times of
LAUREL
─ AND ─
HARDY

Ronald Bergan

This edition first published in 1992 by SMITHMARK Publishers Inc.,
112 Madison Avenue, New York, NY 10016

ISBN 0–8317–5459–1

Consultant editor: Robyn Karney

Design by Millions Design, London

Typeset by Cambrian Typesetters, Frimley, Surrey

Printed and bound in Hong Kong

SMITHMARK books are available for bulk purchase for sales and premium
use. For details write or telephone the Manager of Special Sales,
SMITHMARK Publishers Inc., 112 Madison Avenue, New York, NY 10016.
(212) 532–6600

Picture Credits and Acknowledgements

The publisher would like to thank the following:

Jane Burns and the Stills Department at the BFI

Robert Lewis, President of the Helpmates U.K. Tent of Sons of the Desert,
The Laurel and Hardy Appreciation Society
Helpmates Photo Library
(9, 46, 56, 59, 64–5, 66, 69, 71, 72, 84, 85, 86,
89, 90–1, 92, 97, 98 [2 pictures], 99, 101, 114, 122,
123)

Joel Finler Collection
(11, 19, 36–7, 51, 89, 97, 103, 120)

Gilbert Gibson
Aquarius Picture Library
(12–13, 39, 44–5, 47, 58, 60, 62–3, 70–1, 84, 94–5)

Popperfoto
(107, 110, 112, 113, 115, 118–9)

With special thanks to Guy Callaby

CONTENTS

1   THE THIN ONE AND THE FAT ONE   7

2   LAUREL BEFORE HARDY   13

3   HARDY BEFORE LAUREL   23

4   CHANGING PARTNERS   29

5   HELPMATES   37

6   UNACCUSTOMED AS WE ARE   63

7   MORE NICE MESSES   77

8   BABES IN HOLLYWOOD   95

9   LEAVE 'EM LAUGHING   109

FILMOGRAPHY   124

INDEX   127

THE THIN ONE AND THE FAT ONE

The historic moment when Oliver Hardy as Piedmont Mumblethunder arrives at the dock to meet Stan Laurel as his kilted Scottish nephew in the 1927 short, *Putting Pants on Philip*, was the starting point in the story of the most famous and beloved of all comedy duos in the movies.

Laurel and Hardy were the last arrivals in the Golden Age of screen comedy. Although they had both been in films separately for over a decade, they did not team up officially until the eve of the talkies, coming after Charlie Chaplin, Buster Keaton, Harold Lloyd and Harry Langdon. They also adapted better to sound than the other great comedians of the silent screen. Perhaps this was because their comedy already consisted of giving audiences time to anticipate the next joke. The rest of the comics had to slow down their routine with the coming of sound. As the distinguished American critic Walter Kerr wrote: 'Silent film comedy may be said to have begun in ragtime. Laurel and Hardy turned it back into a stately quadrille.'

Ollie came from playing heavies and Stan from playing the simpleton; put together, these one-dimensional characters grew in humanity, and a genuine inter-relationship was developed, despite the contrasting personalities of the two actors. No matter how much they exasperated one another, their friendship remained unimpaired. 'I'd like you to meet my friend, Mr Laurel,' Ollie would say, and Stan would show the same respect.

On screen Hardy was the dominating partner; off-screen Laurel was the more creative, inventing many of the gags, and contributing to the editing. According to Leo McCarey, who directed them a number of times, 'It was astonishing that Hardy could even find his way to the studio.' Yet it was Stan who took the comic tempo from Ollie.

Once described as 'Dither vs Dignity', they were equal in their stupidity. Ollie was pompous and domineering, with the grand gestures and fine manners of a Southern gentleman who mistakenly believes he is smarter than his foolish partner. It was he who instigated

LEFT AND OVERLEAF
Publicity shots of Stan and Ollie, comedy's most celebrated and enduring partnership.

ABOVE RIGHT
Stan Laurel getting one in the eye from Oliver Hardy's fiddle in Saps at Sea *(1940), although it was usually Ollie, the less brainless of the pair, who would be on the receiving end whenever his mate in mayhem made a move. Ollie may have dominated his partner on screen but it was Stan who was the creative member of the partnership that lasted three decades. Their on-screen relationship remained constant throughout the years.*

RIGHT
Stan's vacant look, later imitated by Jerry Lewis, and Ollie's pompous pose are well caught in the poster for Block-Heads *(1938), one of the boys' last films released by MGM.*

every enterprise, explaining each step (inevitably leading to disaster) to Stan who could never keep up with Ollie's reasoning, but went along with his larger companion all the same.

In their derby hats, wing collars, rumpled but conservative suits and polka-dot ties (Ollie often twiddling his shyly), they were vagrants with bourgeois pretentions. However, despite their deference to authority, their unfailing courtesy, and their reverence for property, they inevitably left a trail of destruction in their wake. 'These two fellows we created, they are nice, very nice people,' Oliver Hardy said. 'They never get anywhere because they are both so very dumb but they don't *know* that they're dumb.'

9

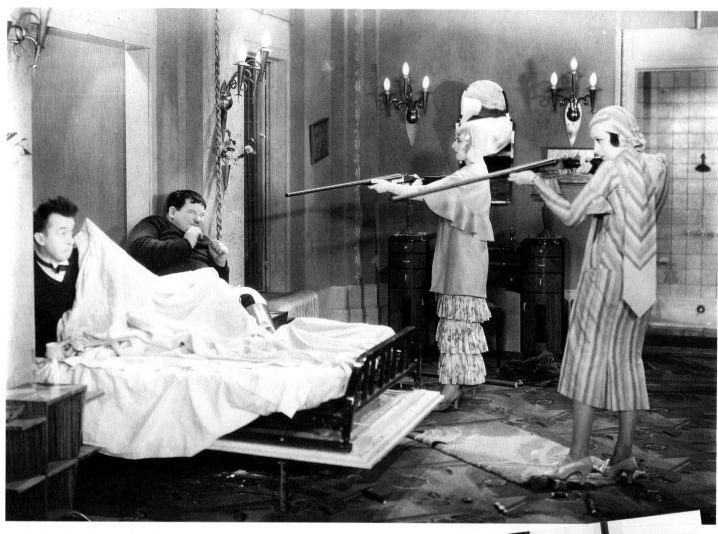

Yet if they had been merely idiots they would never have attracted the love and laughter of generation after generation. Much of their appeal lay in a child-like innocence – children suddenly finding themselves having to behave as adults in a harsh adult world. When Stan cried, he cried not out of anger or hurt, but because he was confused. Even when they played married men, they behaved like naughty boys trying to escape from their nannies.

As film-maker John Grierson commented: 'In this case the meek are not blessed. They do not inherit the earth. They inherit chaos. Chaos most active and violent and diabolical takes advantage of their inhibitions.'

It is hoped that the following pages will go some distance towards answering the questions of how comedy was created out of this chaos, who Stan Laurel and Oliver Hardy really were, and how they differed from Stan and Ollie, two of the most famous comic characters in the history of cinema.

TOP
In **Be Big** *(1931), Stan and Ollie are caught hiding in a wall-bed by their wives (Anita Garvin, right, and Isabelle Keith) after having wrecked the furniture and fittings in their absence.*

ABOVE
In **Hog Wild** *(1930), married men, Stan and Ollie once again behave like naughty boys trying to escape their nannies. In this case, Mrs Hardy (Fay Holderness) has the frying pan.*

RIGHT
Ollie in battered homberg, James Finlayson (centre) in distress, and Charlie Hall (front right) in terror, taken for a ride at a fun-fair by a swirling bevy of lovely flappers in Sugar Daddies (1927), including Stan in drag.

BELOW
The boys, having moved successfully from silent films into sound shorts and features, are seen here behind the camera on the set of Swiss Miss (1938). In reality, Ollie was only interested in acting, while Stan took great pleasure in the creative side of film-making.

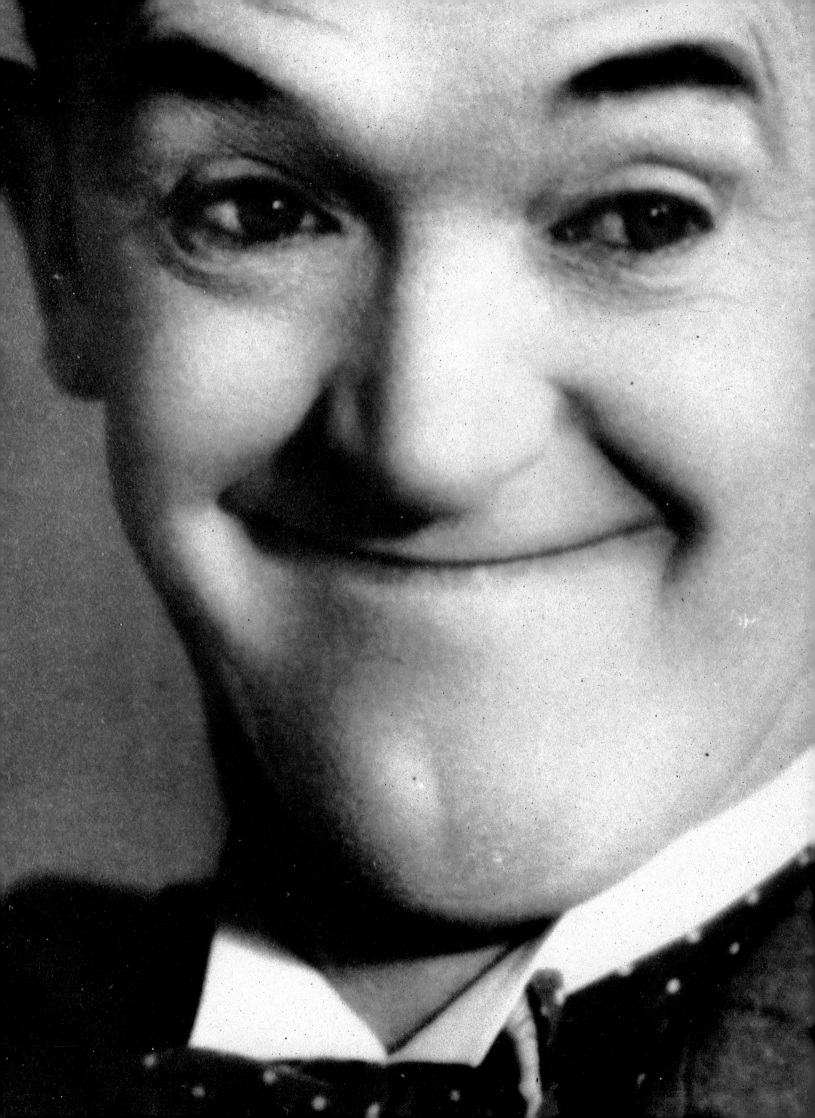

LAUREL
BEFORE HARDY

2

On the 16th of June 1990, the town of Ulverston in Lancashire celebrated the centenary of the birth of its most famous son. Flags were put out, exhibitions were held, films were shown, and visitors came from all over the world to pay homage to the man born Arthur Stanley Jefferson but known universally as Stan Laurel. On the front of 3 Argyle Street is a plaque which reads 'Stan Laurel Was Born In This House 16th June 1890.'

Stan inherited his red hair from his father and his love of show business from both his parents. Producer, actor and playwright Arthur J. Jefferson ran the touring Jefferson Theatre Group. One of its actresses was the beautiful Madge Metcalfe, whom he married. When the troupe ran into difficulties the couple went to live with Madge's parents in Ulverston where Stan was born a few years after his brother Gordon. Later, Stan's younger sister Beatrice arrived, but by then the family had moved to North Shields, where Arthur Jefferson had been appointed manager of the Theatre Royal. Jefferson, who had given up acting for theatre management, was soon to become one of the most renowned impresarios in the north of England, as well as owner of a chain of theatres and managing director of the North British Animated Picture Company.

A. J., as he was called in the business, was a great showman, whose stunts included having a circus cage hauled around the streets with a real lion in it mauling a body. The body was, in fact, a dressed up dummy with a large piece of meat inside. Young Stan was fascinated by the theatre, and spent most of his spare time backstage. When he was sent away to a hated boarding school at Bishop Auckland, he would take every break visiting his father's theatre at North Shields, about thirty miles away. Stan had little interest in learning and wrote to friends many years later about his schooldays:

'I think I have the honour of been [sic] the worst scholar that ever attended there.' A. J. did nothing to discourage his second son from hanging around the theatre, as he hoped he would follow him into management.

After A. J. had lost a great deal of money by investing in the New Theatre Royal in Blythe, which failed to attract enough customers, he gave up all his theatres to manage Glasgow's illustrious Metropole Theatre in 1901. Stan, now sixteen, abandoned his schooling and worked there full-time in the gallery box-office. But his ambition was to perform on stage.

He finally plucked up enough courage to approach Mr Pickard of Pickard's Museum, a Glasgow music hall. 'I'm funny,' the slightly-built young man told Mr Pickard. 'How d'ye know?' asked Pickard. 'Let me on just once, sir, and if I'm not any good, then I shan't pester you any more. But I will be good. You'll see. And if I'm any good, maybe you'll give me a chance at your hall in Clydebank?' Pickard decided to give the young beginner a chance.

'The act was awful, just bloody awful,' Stan recalled to his first biographer John McCabe. 'But I finished strong. And what's more, the applause was very big. I didn't realize that this was because the audience felt sorry for me.' He had not told his father about his debut performance, but coincidentally A. J. chose that night to go to Pickard's and saw his son's act. He decided that if Stan could make it on stage, he would not stand in his way.

Although Stan was close to his father, he adored his mother, whose health was permanently damaged after the birth of another son, Everett.

It was not long before Stan was touring England with Levy and Cardwell's Pantomimes in *Sleeping Beauty*. At a salary of one pound a week, he worked as stage manager and played a Golliwog. The star of the show was Wee Georgie Wood, who made a living playing a child for more than half a century. Stan followed this with appearances in straight plays, one of which was called *Alone in the World*. In it, the adolescent actor was disguised as an old tramp fishing on the banks of the levee in Dixie, with a chorus in the background singing 'Swanee River'. Stan's line was, 'Wall, I guess 'n calculate I cain't ketch no fish with that tarnation mob a-singin. Gee whizz!'

His first big break came when he was offered the chance to join Fred Karno's Army, the most famous troupe of music-hall performers in the country whose star would soon be Charlie Chaplin (whom Stan understudied, besides doing his own turns). One of Karno's most popular shows was called *Mumming Birds*, a burlesque of a typical music-hall bill with some members of the cast playing noisy members of the audience. Stan usually played The Comic Singer who sang an intentionally awful song and who told jokes such as, 'You know the last time I sang this song, a fellow said to me, "You know with your voice you should be with Carl Rosa." "But Carl Rosa's dead," I said. "Yes, I know, that's what I mean!"' Elsewhere in the show, Stan revealed his talent for mime. Many years later Marcel Marceau was to write, 'Stan Laurel was one of the great mimes of our time.'

Mumming Birds was so successful that Karno was invited to take the show to America, where it was presented under the title *A Night in an English Music*

LEFT
Charlie Chaplin (in life-belt), the star of Mumming Birds, *with his understudy, Stan Jefferson, (kneeling, far left), Arthur Dandoe (right of Chaplin), and Fred Karno Jr (left of Chaplin) on their way to America with the Fred Karno troupe aboard the* SS Cairnrona *in 1910. It was the first trip across the Atlantic for Charlie and Stan, who paid a short visit to Hollywood during the tour. They were both back for good two years later.*

Hall. In 1910, Karno's company crossed the Atlantic on the *SS Cairnrona*. As the liner came in sight of Ellis Island, Chaplin declaimed, 'America, I am coming to conquer you! Every man, woman and child shall have this name on their lips – Charles Spencer Chaplin!' Stan had no such grandiose ambitions, although he too was to become a household name.

Charles Chaplin and Stanley Jefferson shared cheap lodgings in New York and on the tour around the USA. Chaplin, a year older than his understudy, and always jealous of rivals, failed to mention Stan in his autobiography. Stan recalled: 'We had a lot of fun in those days. Charlie and I roomed together and I can still see him playing the violin or cello to cover the noise of the cooking of bacon I was doing on the gas ring

LEFT
Charles Spencer Chaplin, in his early 20s, on the brink of realising his dream of conquering America. It would not be long before he adopted the much-loved persona of the Little Tramp in Keystone comedies.

LEFT
Stan set sail for America with Fred Karno's company for the second time in 1912, and was not to return home for twenty years. He formed the Keystone Trio, and the Stan Jefferson Trio, and in 1917, Stan Jefferson became Stan Laurel and appeared in his first film.

RIGHT
Mabel Normand, a brilliant comedienne, starred in a large number of Mack Sennett shorts, eleven of them with Charlie Chaplin. Her career was ruined by the scandal that linked her with the murder of director William Desmond Taylor in 1922. Mabel made her last feature a year later, prior to the forming of the Laurel and Hardy partnership.

(forbidden, of course). Then we'd both take towels and try to blow the smoke out of the window.'

Among the places visited by the troupe was Los Angeles, where more and more films were being made. Neither Chaplin nor Stan thought at that time that they would end up there and earn more money than they had ever dreamed of. Meanwhile, Stan felt that his salary was too low so he demanded a rise. After Karno wired back his refusal from London, Stan left the company in Colorado Springs and, with a loan from A. J., he returned to England.

Once back, Stan paired with Arthur Dandoe, also out of favour with Karno, in a knockabout sketch called *The Rum 'Uns from Rome*. When Dandoe moved on Stan teamed up with Ted Leo and Jim Reed, touring in something called *Fun on the Tyrol*. The act was not a success and Stan was forced to borrow from his older brother, Gordon, who was now manager of the Prince's Theatre, London. Fortunately, Karno was sending *A Night in an English Music Hall* back to the USA and wanted Stan so badly as Chaplin's understudy that he was prepared to increase his salary by five dollars to thirty a week. In 1912, Stan set sail once more. He would not return to England for two decades.

After Mack Sennett, the boss of Keystone Studios, had seen Chaplin in the show and offered him a film contract, the Karno tour quickly folded. But when the troupe returned to England, Stan decided to stay on in America with his own act. He joined ex-Karno husband-and-wife team, Edgar and Wren Hurley, calling them-selves alternately 'The Three Comiques', 'Hurley, Stan and Wren', and 'The Keystone Trio'. Stan used to take off Chaplin, Edgar Hurley did Chester Conklin and Hurley's wife did Mabel Normand. When the trio split up, Stan replaced his partners with Alice Hamilton and Baldwin 'Baldy' Cooke. They formed 'The Stan Jefferson Trio' and played vaudeville theatres through-out America.

In March 1917, the trio was playing at the Hippo-drome Theater in Los Angeles when the producer of the show, Adolph Ramish, suggested to Stan that he had the potential to become a film comedian. 'I've been watching you from the wings,' he said. 'I know,' said Stan. 'Hope you like us.' 'I like *you* all right. It's my personal opinion that you're funnier than Chaplin.' Ramish persuaded former stage comic Robbin 'Bobby' Williamson, director at Kalem Studios, to make a short film with Stan, for which the comic was paid $75 a week. The film was called *Nuts in May* (no copies exist any more), in which Stan played an idiot who wore a Napoleon hat – a frantic slapstick characterisation that bore only a slight resemblance to the clown he was to become. It was shown at the Hippodrome to an audience which included Carl Laemmle, the head of Universal Studios. Laemmle promptly signed Stan to do a string of one-reelers featuring him in the role of Hickory Hiram, a comic rustic. Unfortunately, they were not terribly funny or successful, and Stan's contract with Universal was not renewed.

Also appearing in the 'Hickory Hiram' films was a young Australian actress called Mae Charlotte Dahlberg. The story goes that it was the superstitious Mae who made Stan change his name because Stan Jefferson had thirteen letters in it. Another version is that he decided to change it himself when he saw a picture in a dressing room of a Roman general wearing a laurel wreath, because he thought Stan Laurel would sound funny. He

and Mae then formed a new vaudeville act called Stan and Mae Laurel, giving most people the idea that they were married.

It was Stan who caught the attention of Gilbert M. 'Broncho Billy' Anderson, the predecessor of William S.

Hart as the great screen cowboy, and co-founder of the Essanay Film Company. He hired Stan for a comedy short, *The Lucky Dog* (1917), in which a fat street-thief with a large moustache sticks a Colt .45 in Stan's ribs and says (on the title card), 'Put 'em both up insect before I comb your hair with lead.' Stan despatches the hold-up man with a swift kick on the seat of his pants. The small role was played by a large amiable actor named Oliver Hardy.

MGM-14702

HARDY
BEFORE LAUREL

When Oliver Hardy was a small boy, his mother would occasionally go to fortune-tellers. One day she went to visit a lady in Decatur, Georgia, and the lady told her that her son's name would be known all over the world some time in the future. Mrs Hardy lived to see the prophecy fulfilled.

Oliver Norvell Hardy was a big baby. The youngest of five children, he weighed 14 lbs at his birth in Harlem, Georgia on 18th January 1892. Oliver's sister Elizabeth remembered that he weighed 250 lbs at the age of fourteen. 'He did used to eat a lot as a boy, he was awfully fond of his food.' Oliver Hardy Senior had also been a big man. A lawyer and a leading figure in local politics, he died when Norvell was only eighteen months old. He came from English stock, and claimed to have been a direct descendant of Lord Nelson's famous aide-de-camp, the one whom the admiral asked to kiss him on his death bed. Now a widow, Ollie's mother, née Emily Norvell, of Scottish descent, moved the family to the town of Madison, Georgia where she had bought a small hotel. There the child got into the habit of what he called 'lobby watching' – which is precisely what it was. He would sit in the lobby and watch people. There he saw many Laurel and Hardys. 'I used to see them in my mother's hotel when I was a kid; the dumb, dumb guy who never has anything bad happen to him – and the smart, smart guy who's dumber than the dumb guy only he doesn't know it.'

Blessed with an attractive singing voice, Ollie was permitted to join Coburn's Minstrels as a boy soprano when he was only eight years old. Mrs Hardy wrote to Mr Coburn and he assured her that he would keep a paternal eye on young Norvell. The minstrel show toured all over the South, and the boy made a hit by singing 'Silver Threads Among the Gold' and 'When

You and I Were Young, Maggie'. But after a few months, he grew homesick and returned to his mother's hotel in Madison.

He was then sent to Georgia Military College where he became the butt of jokes about fat boys, although he was always ready with a riposte. Sometimes he was so tired after drilling that he would simply lie down flat on the ground and could not be moved. The headmaster called him 'the funniest boy in the world'. But Ollie was unhappy at the college and ran away, ostensibly because they didn't feed him enough.

At about the same time he became attracted by moving pictures, vaudeville and show people. He was once discovered by his mother singing to illustrated slides for a wage of fifty cents a day in a movie theatre. Because of his voice, he studied singing for a while at Atlanta Conservatory of Music, and it was thought he would make singing his career. But his teacher, Adolph Dahm Peterson, said, 'The young man has a beautiful voice – but no damned ambish!' Later, Ollie went to Georgia State University to study law, and was serious about entering the legal profession. His family's

response was: 'Why, Norvell, you're just a big fat baby. How'd you ever win a law suit?' Both they and he knew that he was destined for some role in show business. While still in his teens, Ollie sang and acted in stock companies, small-time vaudeville and on the showboats that plied American rivers in those days. He also sang in a male quartet called The Twentieth Century Four.

In 1910, when he was eighteen, the Hardy family left Madison for Milledgeville, where Oliver opened his own movie theatre, financed partly by his mother. 'I saw some of the comedies that were being made and I thought to myself that I could be as good – or maybe as bad – as some of those boys,' he later remarked. So, in 1913, he travelled to Jacksonville, Florida, to work as an extra with the Lubin Motion Pictures Company for a few dollars a day. By helping the cameramen, assisting the directors and acting as script-clerk, he learned about all aspects of the business. Gradually, the burly youngster was cast as a 'heavy' in the many one-reelers the Lubin factory churned out. Sporting thick eyebrows, moustache and beard, he was now earning five dollars a day – with three days' work a week guaranteed. He changed his name from Norvell Hardy to Oliver Hardy, although he was always known to his friends and relatives as Babe.

He picked up the nickname from an Italian barber he used to go to near the studio. As Ollie recalled: 'He had

ABOVE
Oliver Hardy playing the heavy in The Perfect Clown *(1926), one of several comedies in which he served as 'second banana' to white-faced Larry Semon (right).*

LEFT
Glum-faced Ollie wears a dunce's hat in an early role.

a thick foreign accent and he was also a boy who liked boys. Well, he took a great fancy to me and every time after he'd finish shaving me, he'd rub powder into my face and pat my cheeks and say, "Nice-a bab-ee. Nice-a babee." The gang used to kid me about it and after a while they started to call me "Baby" and then it was cut down to "Babe" – and I've been Babe Hardy ever since.'

In 1915, Babe made a picture called *The Paper-Hanger's Helper*, in which he played the straight man to comedian Bobby Ray. Ray, a slight man, on the short side, was not dissimilar to Stan Laurel, and the two-reeler had elements of the later Laurel and Hardy movies. But he continued to work mainly as a heavy for Lubin in Florida, while making trips to New York to act with Pathé, Gaumont, Edison, Vitagraph and only one for Gilbert M. 'Broncho Billy' Anderson. It was *The Lucky Dog* (1917) in which he confronted Stan Laurel for the first time.

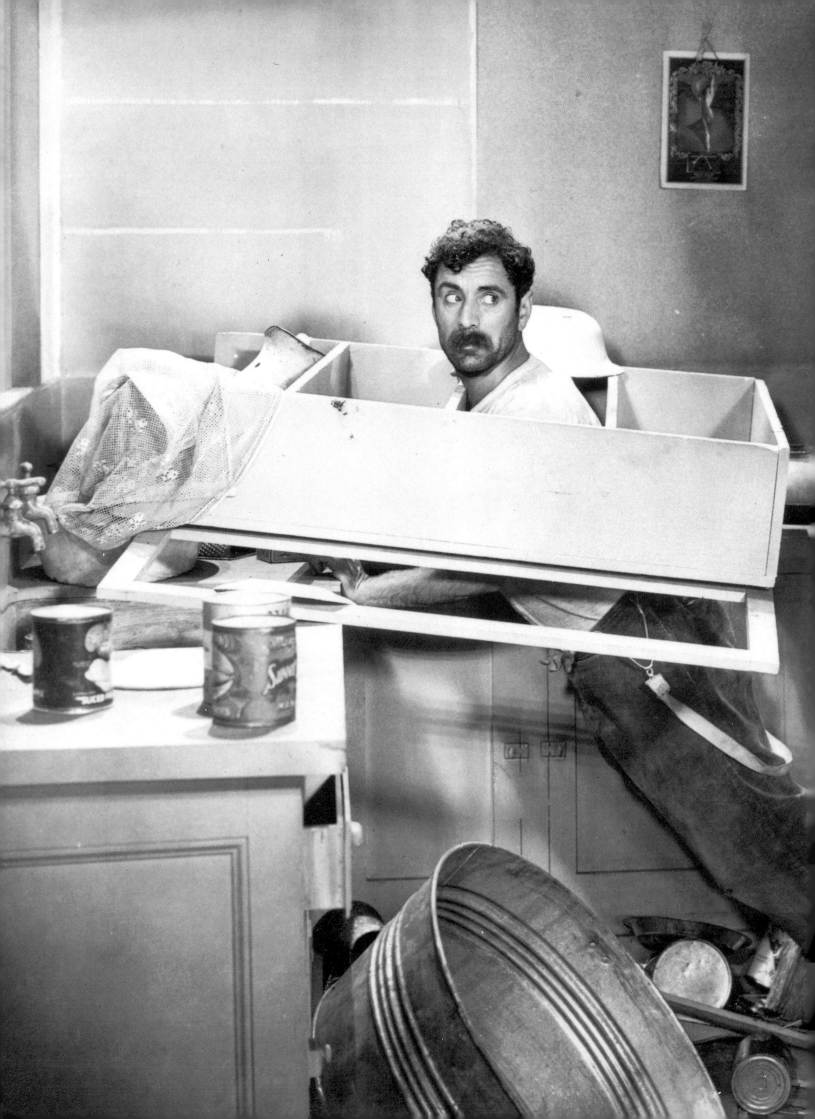

CHANGING PARTNERS

4

The first cinematic meeting between Stan
Laurel and Oliver Hardy in *The Lucky Dog*
gave no indication that they would ever become
partners. 'He and I were just working comics, glad
to have a job – any job,' recalled Stan. So they
went their separate ways again, occasionally
coming together in the same film but not as a
team.

OVERLEAF
Charlie Hall, the boys' perennial victim, suffers once again at their hands in Laughing Gravy *(1931). Stan and Ollie are Hall's tenants, trying to hide a small dog from him.*

RIGHT
Stan as the matador Rhubarb Vaselino in Mud and Sand *(1922), a skit on the Valentino hit of the same year,* Blood And Sand. *It was followed by another parody,* When Knights Were Cold *(1923).*

When the United States entered the war in April 1917, Ollie went along to the local recruiting office. Much to his chagrin, the soldier behind the desk shouted, 'Hey Sarge, come look at what wants to enlist!' When the sergeant appeared, the two men doubled up with laughter. So it was back to the movies where his girth was more appreciated.

Ollie was never out of work. Between 1914 and his eventual teaming with Stan, he made more than two hundred movies, most of them since lost or destroyed. He was much in demand as a heavy in Chaplin-imitator Billy West's comedies, and was offered more money the

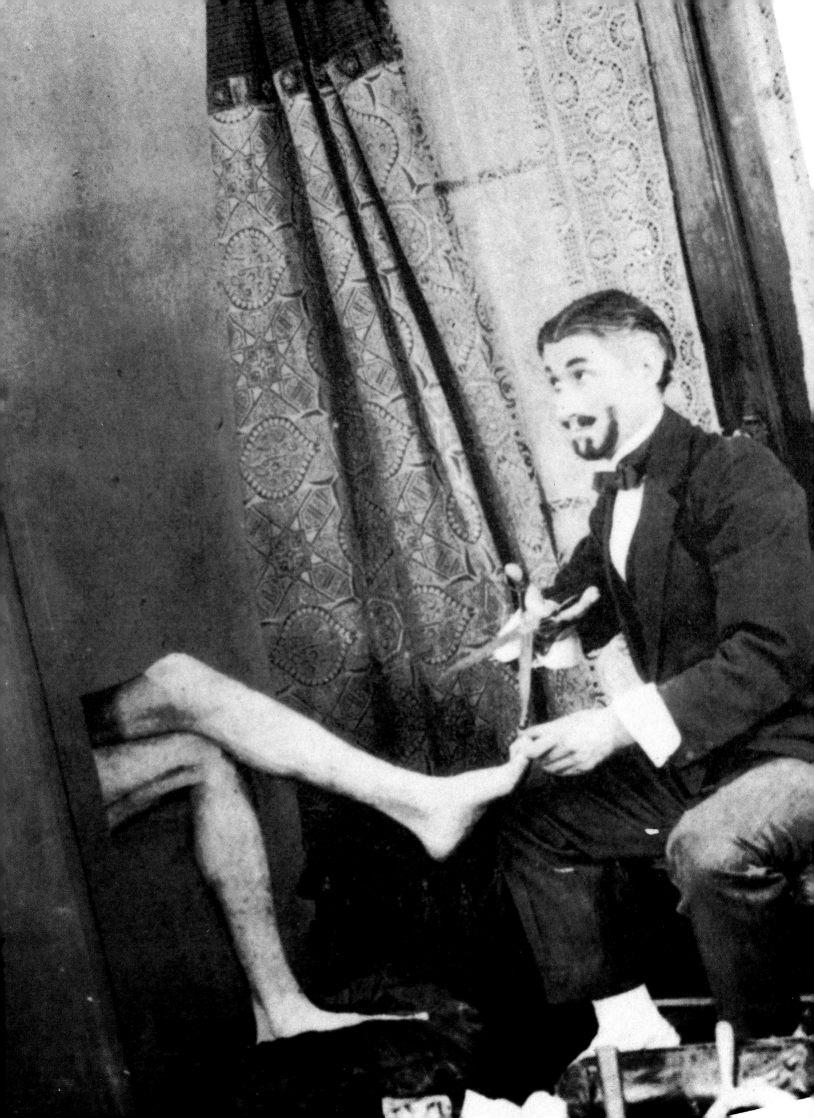

more weight he put on. One of the films, *Playmates* (1918), had Hardy and West as children, a foretaste of the later Laurel and Hardy talkie, *Brats*. At Vitagraph in California, Ollie played foil to Larry Semon in countless short comedies. Semon, one of the most popular and highly paid Hollywood comedians of the early 'twenties, played a white-faced dumbbell with a stupid grin and oversized pants. In one of his last films, he was the Scarecrow accompanied by Ollie as the Tin Woodman in *The Wizard of Oz* (1925). This was the second silent screen version of Frank L. Baum's popular children's classic.

Meanwhile, for 'Broncho Billy' Anderson, Stan was being featured in a number of parodies of popular films of the day. These included *Mud and Sand*, a take-off of Valentino's *Blood and Sand*, in which Stan played matador Rhubarb Vaselino; and *When Knights were Cold* (a skit on Marion Davies' *When Knighthood was in Flower*). Appearing in these with Stan was his vaudeville partner and lover, Mae Dahlberg. They were unable to marry because she already had a husband in Australia, and their relationship was becoming somewhat strained. Stan started to drink heavily, and earned the reputation of being unreliable, but producer Joe Rock nevertheless wanted to hire him – minus Mae, whom he considered crude. She, however, insisted on being in his pictures, so in desperation Rock bought Mae a one-way ticket back to Australia, plus $300 worth of jewelry, $100 for clothes, and $300 in cash. After the initial loneliness, Stan cut down on his drinking and soon found a new love when Rock introduced him to Lois Neilson. They hit it off straight away and were married about six weeks later.

For Rock, Stan continued his burlesques of famous contemporary films such as *The Soilers (The Spoilers)*, *Under Two Jags (Under Two Flags)*, *Rupert of Hee Haw (Rupert of Hentzau)*, *Wild Bill Hiccup (Wild Bill Hickock)*,

LEFT
Stan and Ollie in the 1930s with Hal Roach, the producer who was responsible for bringing the boys together as a team in 1927. Their association was to last thirteen years. In 1967, Roach, aged 75, produced The Crazy World Of Laurel And Hardy.

Monsieur Don't Care (Monsieur Beaucaire) and *Dr Pyckle and Mr Pryde*. When Hal Roach offered Stan a contract with more money than Rock could match, he could not resist.

Roach had begun in films as an actor in 1912 when he met a bit player called Harold Lloyd, whom he thought could become a comedy star. When Roach inherited some money he immediately put Lloyd under contract. After initial disappointments, Lloyd made him rich. Unlike his rival, Mack Sennett, Roach concentrated on strong storylines and well-structured films. His 'Comedy All-Stars' included Snub Pollard, Charley Chase and Our Gang.

At the Roach studio Stan wrote scripts, devised and developed gags and directed. Roach did not allow him to act. A few years earlier, Roach had used Stan to complete a short series of comedies when another star, Toto the clown, had quit. But although Stan performed well, his red hair and light blue eyes photographed so palely on the orthochromatic film that he had to use a great deal of makeup and still looked blind. It was not until the introduction of panchromatic film, which was sensitive to a whole spectrum of colour, that his facial expressions could be shown to advantage on screen.

At the same time Roach had hired Oliver Hardy to work on several movies. Two of these, *Yes, Yes, Nanette!* (1925) and *Enough To Do* (1926), were directed by Stan. On the domestic front, Ollie had married Myrtle Lee Reeves in 1925, but his new wife took exception to his passionate interest in golf, horse-racing and card-playing. He was a gregarious and jolly man, whom everyone liked, but it was not long before his marriage was heading for the rocks.

In 1926, Ollie was playing a butler in *Get 'Em Young*, which Stan was directing. One day however, Ollie, a good cook as well as a gourmet, scalded himself badly with boiling fat while roasting a leg of lamb, and Stan had to take over in the role. It was in this picture that he first introduced his celebrated whimpering cry. 'In the film, I was a very timid chap, running around and reacting with horror to everything that went on around me,' explained Stan. 'To emphasize this, I cried at one point, screwed my face up – and have used it ever since. Funny thing about that cry, though: it's the only mannerism I ever used in the films that I didn't like.'

One of Ollie's famous bits of business occurred in *Sailors Beware!* In it, he plays a rough sea captain who kidnaps a young lady, taking her to his ship. Stan, the girl's lover, gets on board disguised as a Theda Bara-type vamp, to whom the captain makes advances until his large wife appears. Stan then escapes with the girl. In one scene Ollie has a bucket of water thrown over him. 'There were some ladies watching us. So I waved the tie in a kind of tiddly-widdly fashion, in a kind of comic way, to show that I was embarrassed,' recalled Hardy. 'I

improved on that little bit of business later on, and I used it for any number of situations. But usually I did it when I had to show extreme embarrassment while trying to look friendly at the same time.' In the same film, he used what was to be another trademark – his famous exasperated stare at the camera.

Stan was now back as a performer, and Roach put Stan and Ollie together in a film version of an old music hall sketch called *Duck Soup*. *Slipping Wives*, of the same year, was the story of an artist, his wife, and her lover –

BELOW
Oliver Hardy demonstrating the celebrated 'twiddling and widdling' of his tie for the public who expected it of him wherever he went. The mannerism was derived from a character in Sailors Beware! *(1927).*

the latter a paint salesman played by Stan. Ollie took the role of the comic butler. Eight more films followed, including *Sailors Beware!*, by the completion of which a new era was beginning for the thirty-seven-year-old Stan Laurel and the thirty-five-year-old Oliver Hardy.

Just as audiences began to expect certain bits of business from Hardy, they would wait for Laurel to deliver his whimpering cry when things got too much for him. Here he is seen as the familiar cry baby in A Chump at Oxford *(1940).*

ABOVE
Unlike Stan, whose background lay in music hall with the Karno company and vaudeville in America, Ollie's training was mostly in films.

5 HELPMATES

The title of *Putting Pants on Philip* refers to the attempt of Piedmont Mumblethunder (Hardy) to see that his kilted Scottish nephew Philip (Laurel) conforms in dress to the other male members of the American small town where Piedmont has some standing. Before the offending kilt can be replaced, Philip chases every pretty girl in sight, is affected by upward draughts of air from sidewalk gratings, and even loses his underwear. After he is fitted with a pair of trousers, Philip lays his kilt on the ground to allow a girl to step safely across a puddle in the street. When she refuses the offer, Piedmont sees his chance to ruin the offending garment for ever by stepping on it, only to find himself sinking up to his neck in mud.

OVERLEAF
Ollie biting the hand that feeds him in Early to Bed *(1928), in which he has inherited a fortune and lords it over Stan. The latter decides to wreck the mansion.*

BELOW
Piedmont Mumblethunder (Hardy) measuring his reluctant Scottish nephew (Laurel) for a pair of trousers in Putting Pants on Philip *(1927); the beginning of a perfect partnership.*

lthough it took a few more films to develop the fixed personalities that Laurel and Hardy would be loved and acclaimed for, it was clear that *Putting Pants On Philip* was the beginning of a perfect comic partnership – the fat Ollie displaying his pomposity and outraged dignity, and the thin Stan innocently unaware of the havoc his idiocy causes.

Walter Kerr described the scene in which Philip is measured for a pair of trousers thus: 'Deeply virginal, immensely shy of the tailor's attentions as the measuring tape is applied to his leg. Laurel recoils, near tears, with each overture. Alert as he is to the tailor's unspeakable intentions, his eyes are sleepier now, glazed with injury;

his hair, no longer sleeked down, stands on end like a field of alfalfa, hinting fright. The fact that the assault is taken as homosexual and Laurel doesn't even know what homosexuality *is* is simply an indication that the once knowing and aggressive Laurel is becoming as childlike as Roach envisioned.'

The film was supervised by Leo McCarey, directed by Clyde A. Bruckman, and photographed by George Stevens. It was McCarey, (the future director of The Marx Brothers in *Duck Soup* (1933) and Bing Crosby in *Going My Way* (1944)), who 'discovered' Laurel and Hardy. He recognised that the way to bring out the best in their act was to slow the pace down – a daring innovation at that period of frenetic comedy. 'We're all working too fast,' he said. 'We've got to get away from these jerky movements and work out at normal speed.'

Therefore, in the succeeding films, the pair gave themselves time to develop the situations and characters. Unlike many of the other screen comedians of the day, they were not outlandishly dressed or social outcasts, but 'ordinary' members of the community – builders, salesmen, servants, sailors, detectives – wearing derby

LEFT
Scottish once again, McLaurel and Hardy survey a snuff box and a set of bagpipes they have inherited in Bonnie Scotland *(1935), one of their first features.*

ABOVE
Stan Laurel and Oliver Hardy in different guises, as foreign legionnaires, solid citizens and sailor boys – 'ordinary' members of the community.

hats, conservative suits, high collars and polka-dot ties, trying to find acceptance in society. Because they were never able to do so, a vast section of their audiences, especially during the Depression, were able to identify with them. The humour came from the fact that they were both dumb, but didn't *know* they were dumb; and from the way they always attempted to retain their

dignity in the most undignified circumstances. Though there were still traces of the white-faced clown and vaudeville comedian in Stan's character, it had been humanised to portray the child in us all. Ollie had partly derived his screen persona from a comic strip character in the Georgia newspapers called Helpful Henry who, according to the actor, 'was always trying to be helpful

but he was always making a mess of things. He was very big and fussy and important but underneath it all, he was a very nice guy.'

In the films following *Putting Pants on Philip*, a more or less stock Laurel and Hardy company emerged, led by James Finlayson, Charlie Hall, Edgar Kennedy, Mae Busch and Anita Garvin. Born in Falkirk, Scotland in 1887, Finlayson, known as Fin to everybody in the business, made over thirty films with the duo beginning with *Love 'Em and Weep* (1927). With a ferocious squint, bald and moustached, Fin was noted for his explosive nature, horrendous mugging, and what he called his 'double take and fade away' when faced with some appalling idiocy perpetrated by Stan and Ollie. This mannerism consisted of a double take embellished by wide circlings and twistings of the head, and concluding with the head thrown back violently as the right eye closed and the left eyebrow rose impossibly high.

Former Karno trouper Charlie Hall appeared in around forty-seven pictures with the boys, usually as a heavy with an ability to take punishment while showing frustrated anger, unlike bald-headed Edgar Kennedy, who was the master of the 'slow burn'. Of the women in the movies, generally treated misogynistically, Australian-born Mae Busch stands out, usually playing Ollie's harridan wife, an effective contrast to the sexier Anita Garvin.

In *The Second Hundred Years* (1927), James Finlayson is the irascible governor of a prison in which Stan and Ollie are serving sentences that are so long, that when

ABOVE
Anita Garvin (in striped dress) as the long-suffering Mrs Laurel (Isabelle Keith is Mrs Hardy) in Be Big *(1931). The attractive, green-eyed, brunette had been a Ziegfeld girl before going into the movies in 1925, aged 18.*

LEFT
The irascible, cock-eyed Scot, James Finlayson, on the receiving end in Big Business *(1929). 'Fin' was the best-known member of the Laurel and Hardy Stock Company.*

FAR LEFT
Mae Busch as the blackmailing old flame of married man Hardy in Chickens Come Home *(1931). Australian-born Mae, who appeared in almost a dozen films with the duo, often played Ollie's harridan wife, and the occasional vamp. She died in 1946.*

another prisoner announces he still has a stretch of forty years to go, Stan hands him a letter to post when he gets out. Their first attempt to escape through a tunnel fails when they come up in the warden's office. At a second attempt, they leave through the main gates, disguised as painters. Stan and Ollie then steal the car and clothes of some Frenchmen, who turn out to be visitors of the governor (Finlayson), and the pair end up back within the prison walls. The boys' act does not fool anyone for long. After a dinner party in which their unorthodox table manners cause raised eyebrows, especially from Finlayson, their brief taste of freedom is ended.

For their roles as convicts, both comedians had had their heads shaved. When Stan's hair began to grow

ABOUT
Stan and Ollie, still shaven-headed from the jail movie, The Second Hundred Years, *seen here with Charley Chase and James Finlayson in* Call of the Cuckoos *(1927).*

RIGHT
A poster for the first compilation of silent comedy, a revelation for audiences in 1957. Stan and Ollie are pictured in a scene from The Second Hundred Years *(1927).*

again, he found it difficult to brush it back, and it stuck up in a way that caused laughter among his friends and colleagues. He therefore decided to keep it that way for the act, emphasising the look by scratching his head and pulling up of the hair simultaneously.

He used this gesture in *Hats Off* (1927), in which he and Ollie are struggling to haul a bulky washing-machine up a long flight of stairs, a situation they used again, with variations and to greater effect, in one of their most famous shorts, *The Music Box* in 1932. In

"The Greatest List of
Star Comedians Ever!"
—N. Y. *Daily News*

LAUREL & HARDY
WILL ROGERS
JEAN HARLOW
CAROLE LOMBARD
BEN TURPIN
HARRY LANGDON

RELEASED BY
WENTIETH CENTURY-FOX

Produce

TH

58/106
Printed in U. S. A.

44

Getting a little behind in his work

GOLDEN AGE of COMEDY

OBERT YOUNGSON Winner of 2 Academy Awards and 6 Academy Award Nominations

ABOVE
Laurel and Hardy pretending to sneak out on their boss Hal Roach at the Roach studios. There certainly were many occasions when they would have liked to have set up their own company.

RIGHT AND OVERLEAF
The gigantic pie-throwing final sequence of The Battle of the Century (1927). Actually, the film's title refers to boxer Stan's few minutes in the ring in the first reels of the film.

1927, one of the Roach ideas men was driving through the Hollywood Hills section of L.A., when he noticed a very steep stairway leading from the main street to a house high up on one of the hills, and he thought it might be used for a comedy.

Most of the gags for the pictures were developed by the producer (usually Roach himself), the director (Fred L. Guiol, Clyde A. Bruckman, James Parrott or Leo McCarey) and Stan. Ollie was usually absent on the golf course. 'I have never really worked hard in the creation department,' he told John McCabe. 'After all, just *doing* the gags is hard enough work, especially if you've taken so many falls and been dumped in as many mudholes as I have.' In fact, knowing that Ollie was always impatient

to get out on the golf course or go racing, Stan would sometimes hold up the shooting to get a genuinely exasperated look out of his partner.

Among the thirteen shorts they made in 1927, *The Battle of the Century* is famous for providing the most gigantic pie-throwing scene in cinema history. The pie in the face had been a standby of silent comedy ever since Mabel Normand threw a custard pie at Fatty Arbuckle in *A Noise from the Deep* back in 1913. The idea for *The Battle of the Century* came about during a session where the gag men were sitting around discussing a plot for a new Laurel and Hardy picture. As it seemed a bit thin, someone suggested embellishing it with some pie-throwing. This was hooted down as

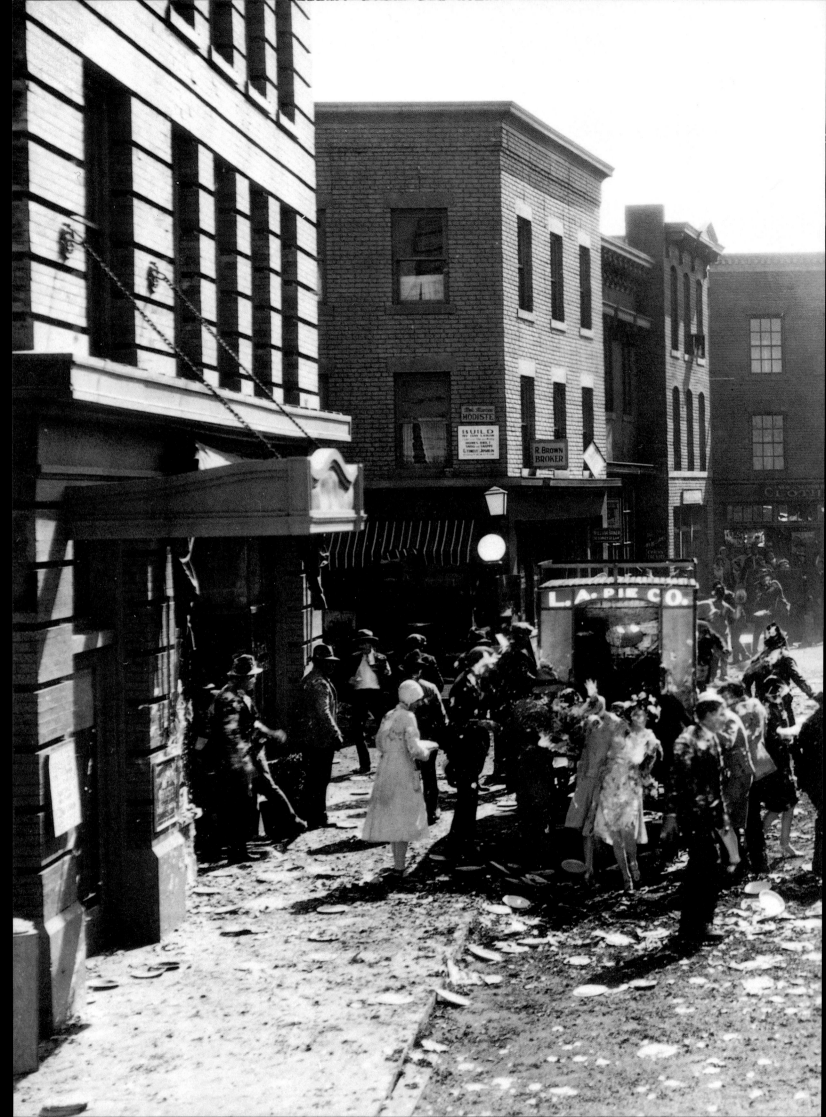

being old hat, until Stan said: 'Look, if we make a pie picture – let's make a pie picture to end all pie pictures. Let's give them so many pies that there will never be room for any more pie pictures in the whole history of movies.' As a result, a multitude of pies were thrown at the climax – custard pies, blueberry pies, raspberry, coconut, banana and lemon cream pies, all of them real and supplied by the L. A. Pie Company. Henry Miller, the author of *Tropic of Cancer* and *Tropic of Capricorn*, wrote in 1945: 'This, in my opinion, is the greatest comic film ever made – because it brought the pie-throwing to apotheosis. There was nothing but pie-throwing in it, nothing but pies, thousands and thousands of pies and everybody throwing them right and left.' However, Miller did not remember that the sequence is only the last third of the film. Leading up to the pie-filled finale is the story of a prizefighter (Stan) and his manager (Ollie). After Stan is knocked cold with one blow, Ollie decides that money must be found elsewhere. When he is offered the chance to cash in on insurance money if Stan meets with an accident, he decides to help matters along. Stan fails to slip on a banana skin which Ollie repeatedly throws in front of

him, but a pieman (Charlie Hall), coming along carrying a large tray of pies, does. Charlie pushes a pie in Ollie's face, Ollie retaliates, and finally the whole street is involved.

In 1928, Laurel and Hardy made eleven pictures, starting with *Leave 'Em Laughing* which, despite being a silent film, was based on the assumption that laughter is contagious. Ollie and Stan are accidentally exposed to laughing gas at the dentist, and continue to laugh in the street and in their Tin Lizzie. When they are confronted with a glowering traffic cop (Edgar Kennedy), they cannot control their hilarity, and eventually the whole street is roaring with laughter. What makes the film so funny is watching the variety of facial expressions involved in the act of laughing. 'At one time we actually had to stop shooting one day because we were laughing so much,' Stan recalled. 'I broke up Babe, and he broke me up. We finally had to call it a day when it got too much for us.'

The Finishing Touch had Stan and Ollie as jobbing builders, hired to finish off a half-built house. They finish it off alright when, after throwing bricks and rocks at each other, their truck rolls down a hill and

FAR LEFT
Cop Edgar Kennedy fails to see the joke in Leave 'Em Laughing *(1928). Kennedy, the master of the 'slow burn', directed two of the boys' films,* From Soup To Nuts *and* You're Darn Tootin' *(both 1928).*

LEFT
As jobbing builders, Stan and Ollie keep their hats on with their overalls while destroying the house they were employed to build in The Finishing Touch *(1928).*

Laurel and Hardy wait to be admitted to the house of socialite Mrs Culpepper in From Soup to Nuts *(1928), where they have been hired to serve at dinner. Low comedy in high society ensues.*

flattens the house at the bottom. One of the rocks they threw was there to prevent the truck moving! In *From Soup to Nuts*, they are hired to serve at a high society dinner party thrown by Mrs Culpepper (Anita Garvin), of whom the opening title reads: 'Mrs Culpepper is an idol of the snobs – and a pain in the neck to everybody else.' Needless to say, the pair reduce the evening to a shambles, especially when Stan misunderstands the instruction to serve the salad 'undressed'.

Leo McCarey, the director of the movie, explained how a favourite moment came about. 'One day Babe was playing the part of a *maitre d'* coming in to serve a cake. He steps through the doorway, falls and finds himself on the floor, his head buried in the cake. I shouted, 'Don't move! Just don't move! Stay like that.' Hardy stayed still stretched out, furious, his head in the cake – you could only see his back. And for a minute and a half, the audience couldn't stop laughing.'

Edgar Kennedy directed *You're Darn Tootin'*, featuring Stan and Ollie as clarinettist and horn-player respectively in an orchestra whose conductor they drive crazy, particularly when Stan sends the music stands falling like dominoes. Fired, they return to their lodgings where, during the meal, Ollie empties an entire salt cellar into his soup after Stan has left the cap loose.

BELOW
A street fight, provoked by buskers Stan and Ollie in You're Darn Tootin' *(1928), leaves everyone trouserless, save Laurel for the moment. The duo exit in one pair of pants removed from a very fat man.*

LEFT
Ollie has just emptied the entire contents of the salt cellar into his soup thanks to Stan's incompetence in You're Darn Tootin'. After Stan has performed with the pepperpot, Ollie makes sure he gets to the ketchup bottle to prevent another mishap.

Due to Stan's incompetence the contents of the pepper-pot land in Ollie's soup as well. They then go busking and somehow provoke a fight in which, once again, everybody in the street participates.

In *Wrong Again*, Stan and Ollie, who are working at a stable, hear that the famous 'Blue Boy' has been stolen, and a huge reward is offered for its return. They think they've found it when they see a horse by the same name as the Gainsborough painting, and take it to the owner's mansion. The man, upstairs, tells them to put it on the piano. When he discovers the horse in his living room he chases them away with a shotgun. Whether coincidental or not, the image of the horse on the piano was similar to that of dead donkeys lying on two pianos in *Un Chien Andalou*, a surrealist French film made by Luis Buñuel and Salvador Dali around the same time.

Two Tars was the first of the Laurel and Hardy movies to contain a reciprocal destruction scene. It occurs when the boys, as sailors on shore leave, crash their rented car into one driven by Edgar Kennedy, after which each takes turns in causing damage to the other's vehicle. *Big Business* had more escalating mutual destruction of property. This time, Stan and Ollie are selling Christmas trees door-to-door in midsummer! Havoc ensues when they call at the house of Jimmy Finlayson who slams the door in their faces. Despite this negative response, they persist. This leads to Finlayson cutting their tree to pieces with clippers, their tearing out his doorbell, his attacking their car, their breaking down his front door, his ruining all their trees, and their smashing his windows. Each party stands aside and watches in turn as the other commits a further outrage. But just as it seems that it will end with everyone in tears, Stan hands James Finlayson an exploding cigar and he and Ollie have the last laugh.

Interspersed with the Laurel and Hardy shorts in which they seem to be bachelors, are those in which one or both of them are married. As a caption on one of the films indicates: 'Mr Hardy was married – Mr Laurel was also unhappy.' In private life, both were involved in extra-marital affairs. Ollie had sought escape from a heavy-drinking Myrtle in the arms of Viola Morse.

BELOW
Which of the three sailors is the most intelligent? Stan and Ollie manage to make a fine mess of their shore leave in* Two Tars *(1928), ending up in an orgy of tit-for-tat destruction.

Stan's affair with a married woman remained more discreet. But although his marriage had its ups and downs, it was relatively stable. Lois and Stan now had a daughter, also called Lois, born in 1928.

We Faw Down and *Their Purple Moment* revealed them as married men scheming to outwit their shrewish wives; both movies were forerunners of one of their

BELOW AND RIGHT
At five months old, daughter Lois (below) is not yet appreciative of father Stan's humour, nor was she much impressed by his hounds (right) at the age of five in the gardens of the Laurels' home in Hollywood.

best-loved sound features, *Sons of the Desert* (1933). In *We Faw Down*, the lads try to get to a poker game without their wives knowing by pretending to be going to the theatre. On their return, while answering their spouses questions on the play, they notice a headline in the newspaper that the theatre had burned down earlier that evening. *Their Purple Moment* finds them innocently involved with two floozies at a night-club when their wives turn up. This was the stuff of countless vaudeville farces, but made new by the flawless clowning of Laurel and Hardy.

Stan was often called upon to put on drag *in extremis*. In *That's My Wife*, Ollie asks him to impersonate his wife because she has left him, and a visiting rich uncle plans to hand over a large sum of money to what he

ABOVE
Stan, pressed into posing as Ollie's spouse in That's my Wife (1929), in a wig borrowed from a doll, finds dancing at a smart nightclub full of pitfalls. It all goes terribly wrong when they get involved with a jewel thief and a drunk.

RIGHT
Drag has a long and honourable tradition in comedy and Stan's few appearances in women's clothes were always hilarious such as here in Jitterbugs (1943), the best of Laurel and Hardy's final films. Vivian Blaine is the other woman.

believes are his happily married relatives. Mistaken identity was used again in *Double Whoopee*. When Stan and Ollie arrive at a smart hotel they are mistaken for visiting dignitaries and are greeted effusively by the manager. Faced with the hotel register, Ollie slowly and pompously removes his gloves, delicately takes the pen in his hand and after a few signatures in the air, signs his name ceremoniously. The manager is suitably impressed until he discovers that they are the new doorman and footman.

Double Whoopee is also remembered for one of the first screen appearances of the original Blonde Bombshell, Jean Harlow. Ollie, splendidly decked out in his doorman's uniform, opens a cab door for her to alight, while Stan accidentally closes the door so that the entire

back of her dress is ripped off. She then enters the hotel lobby haughtily, unaware that her delicious rear and beautiful legs have been exposed.

The seventeen-year-old Harlow also appeared as Edgar Kennedy's wife in *Bacon Grabbers*, in which Stan and Ollie are hired to collect goods from people who have fallen behind with their instalment payments. After they repossess a radio from Kennedy, it is crushed by a steamroller. Kennedy finds this hilarious until his wife announces she has just paid for it. It is Stan and Ollie's turn to laugh until the same steamroller flattens their car. Tragically, the lovely Jean Harlow died prematurely only eight years later.

Bacon Grabbers was released with music and effects, as was *Angora Love*, in which Stan and Ollie try in every conceivable way to conceal a goat from their landlord (Edgar Kennedy). These were the last of Laurel and Hardy's silent movies. After *The Jazz Singer* opened in October 1927, the studios could no longer ignore the fact that sound had come to stay. It was not long before Hal Roach decided to make only talking features, but he did continue for a while with silent shorts. Stan and Ollie seemed to feel there was no reason to change their winning formula and try to adapt their style of comedy to sound. Chaplin, in fact, resisted sound for thirteen years after it became current in the cinemas of the world. What many comics feared was that a reliance on spoken dialogue would limit their universal appeal. Although many of today's *aficionados* consider the best Laurel and Hardy period the one which led up to the advent of sound, the duo, as it turned out, need not have worried about meeting the new challenge.

FAR LEFT, ABOVE
Stan and Ollie find themselves elevated to doorman and footman at a smart hotel in Double Whoopee (1929). The hotel manager is unctious until he realized the boys are his new employees and not V.I.P.s. In this shot they are having trouble with the lift.

FAR LEFT
Jean Harlow arrives at the hotel, and Stan and Ollie inadvertently expose the rear of the platinum blonde, in one of her very first screen appearances. She was to die tragically young at the age of 26.

LEFT
The boys, forced to hide their pet goat from the landlord in Angora Love (1929), decide the only way to get rid of its unmistakable smell is to bath it. Easier said than done!

UNACCUSTOMED AS WE ARE

6

The day finally dawned when Stan Laurel and Oliver Hardy had to stand up and be heard. To celebrate the coming of sound, MGM (which distributed Hal Roach's films) put almost all their stars into *Hollywood Revue of 1929* – Marion Davies, Norma Shearer, John Gilbert, Joan Crawford and Lionel Barrymore – with Buster Keaton, Jack Benny and Laurel and Hardy providing the laughs. Although Stan and Ollie spoke, not much dialogue was needed for the eight-minute sequence in which they appeared as maladroit magicians. The act ended with the oldest gag in the business – a pie meant for Stan lands in the face of master of ceremonies Jack Benny. If this was anything to go by, the duo were not going to let sound cramp their comedy style.

OVERLEAF
It was the case that one of the boys never suffered without the other. As buskers, they were down on their luck as usual in Below Zero (1930).

Posters designed to appeal to non-English speaking audiences who had no problem understanding their idols before the talkies. To retain Laurel and Hardy's international reputation, multiple versions of their movies were made in foreign languages. Dubbing would have cost less, but filmgoers abroad wanted to hear the boys' own voices. Sometimes continental actresses replaced American ones.

Actually, the boys' transition to sound was a smooth one, unlike that suffered by Harry Langdon, Buster Keaton and Harold Lloyd. In fact, sound brought an extra dimension to the characters, with the addition of Stan's light Lancashire accent and high-pitched baby cry, and Ollie's singsong, slightly Southern tones, uttering the catch phrase, 'Well, here's another nice mess you've gotten me into.' (Often misquoted as *fine* mess.) Without sound, audiences would have been deprived of their musical numbers and their famous theme tune, 'The Cuckoo Song', composed by T. Marvin Hatley, the musical director at the Hal Roach Studios. It introduced all their films from 1930 onwards, and later was dubbed onto the silent shorts. Hatley also wrote 'Honolulu Baby' for *Sons of the Desert* (1933), and 'Won't You Be My Lovey Dovey' for *Way Out West* (1937).

At the beginning some intertitles were retained, but these were gradually phased out. Of course, Roach was aware that as the films were in English he might lose a fair portion of the world market. In an effort to counteract this, French, Spanish, German and Italian versions of many of the pictures were made, sometimes substituting the supporting cast with native speakers. This meant that each film had to be made five times, with Stan and Ollie reading the languages phonetically from large boards placed strategically around the set.

The first Laurel and Hardy talkie was appropriately titled *Unaccustomed As We Are* (1929). Mae Busch played Mrs Hardy again. She (understandably) walks out on her husband when he brings Stan home to dinner. Hearing of this, Ollie's neighbour, a cop's wife (Thelma Todd), offers to cook for them. In a mishap typical of those which happen when Stan's around, her dress gets burned and she is forced to hide in a trunk when Mrs Hardy and the cop (a seething Edgar Kennedy) appear on the scene.

It hardly differed from any of their silent pictures, although there was an imaginative sound effect when Stan tumbled down the stairs. (It was one of six shorts Lewis R. Foster directed for the team.) 'I thought then

that there was nothing funny about a guy falling downstairs,' explained Stan. 'There's pain connected with it and that's never funny. I realized, of course, that you can take away the sting by not having the man really hurt, but there's nothing real about that. In that scene we removed the pain by having the camera stay looking at the top of the staircase. The sound effect of the fall lets the audience visualize its own scene, and that just makes it funnier to them.'

The Film Exhibitor's Herald reporting on *The Perfect Day* (1929) wrote: 'In one spot Hardy hits Laurel over the head with an automobile jack and the noise from the blow sounded like the ringing of an anvil when struck with a twelve-pound hammer. It is the funniest sound effect yet recorded.'

The Perfect Day concerned Stan and Ollie's fruitless attempts to leave for a picnic in the country in their Tin Lizzie with their wives and Ollie's grumpy uncle (Edgar Kennedy), whose gouty foot is bandaged. With the whole neighbourhood watching they wave goodbye,

only to get a puncture immediately. When they finally depart, after a series of trials and tribulations, they travel just a short way before the car sinks slowly into a mud hole in the road.

So much damage is done to the Model-T Fords in Laurel and Hardy movies that a full stable of them was kept on the lot. Some were completely wrecked and used at the end of a destructive sequence; others were held together by wire so that they could be taken apart section by section. One was squeezed into an accordion shape, and another was sliced in half.

Berth Marks has Stan and Ollie on a train bound for Pottsville, where they are due to appear at a local vaudeville theatre. When they retire for the night to the sleeping car where they naturally (for them) share a

BELOW
Stan on the set of The Perfect Day *(1929), which was directed by James Parrott. Parrott, comedian Charley Chase's brother, directed 20 of the duo's best shorts.*

RIGHT
Waking up to the fact they have arrived at their destination, the boys beat a hasty retreat in their long-johns and derbies in Berth Marks *(1929).*

Ollie ends up holding the baby in Their First Mistake **(1932), while Stan clutches a bottle ready to feed it. The situation has come about because Ollie, hoping to improve his marriage, decides to** **adopt a baby, only to find that his wife (Mae Busch) has left him. In this shot, showing the boys on the set, Ollie has his hands full with the two infants playing the adopted baby.**

single berth, they attempt to get undressed in the cramped space. By the time they have managed to get into their pyjamas, the train has reached Pottsville. The fact that the two friends often share a bed has prompted some critics to find undertones of homosexuality in their relationship, but this is to ignore the traditional nature of clowns, who have often worked in pairs since ancient Greek times. It also ignores the sublime innocence of the period of cinema in which Laurel and Hardy operated. The following extract from *Their First Mistake* (1932) could only have been written and played

with ingenuousness. Mrs Hardy (Mae Busch) has just given Ollie a hiding with a broom. Stan is lying on his bed, and Ollie comes to sit on it.

Stan: What did she say?
Ollie: You heard what she said!
Stan: Well, what's the matter with her, anyway?
Ollie: Oh, I don't know. She says that I think more of you than I do of her.
Stan: Well, you do, don't you?
Ollie: Well, we won't go into that!

Mind you, women are not always absent, neither are they necessarily shrews or vamps. In *Men O'War* (1929) the boys, as sailors on leave, meet two pretty girls in the park. They invite the girls for a soda but, because they only have fifteen cents between them, Ollie takes Stan aside and explains his strategy. 'Now, look, Stanley. We've got just enough money for three glasses of soda pop. I'll ask the girls what they want, I'll take soda, and when I ask you what you want, you say, "I don't want anything, thank you." OK?' 'Sure,' says Stan. After all this, when Stan is asked what he will have, he replies, 'I'll have soda too, thank you.' They compromise by deciding to share a drink. When Stan puts his straw into the glass and drinks it all up, Ollie heaves a massive sigh and looks at the camera. 'Now, why did you do that?' he asks. Stan begins to weep. 'I couldn't help it. My half was on the bottom!' Finally, they are handed a bill by the soda-jerk (James Finlayson) which comes to thirty cents. Luckily, Stan hits the jackpot on a fruit machine. They then take the girls rowing . . . with the expected results.

In 1930, Roach provided MGM with seven Laurel and Hardy shorts, most of them excellent, some of them departing a good way from formula. Leo McCarey and Hal Roach came up with a screenplay for *Brats* in which Stan and Ollie play their own little sons. For the illusion to work, the studio built a larger-than-life set for the duo in kiddie's clothes to romp about it. The use of double-exposure allowed Stan and Ollie to appear in the same frame as their younger selves.

In *Brats*, there is a good illustration of Ollie's superior manner. He takes a glass of water from Stan saying, 'Give it to me. *You* might spill it!', and then opens the door of the kids' bathroom only to topple backwards in a flood of water.

Hog Wild was one of the best demonstrations of the boys' constant battle with inanimate objects. The British documentary film-maker Basil Wright described it thus: 'In this film, the attempt to fix a wireless aerial on the

ABOVE
Ollie gets a withering squinting look from soda-jerk James Finlayson while entertaining Anne Cornwall and Gloria Greer in Men O' War *(1929). They are soon to leave poor Stan to settle the bill which comes to far more than he has in his bell-bottoms.*

LEFT
Stan and Ollie with Lewis R. Foster (with mega-phone) on the set of Men O' War, *posing for a publicity shot. Principally a gag writer and script supervisor, Foster directed six Laurel and Hardy shorts.*

roof of Hardy's house precipitated Hardy off the roof into a goldfish pond at least five times. Each time a different gag-variation appeared, until the comedy passed into the realm of cutting, and the final fall was but a flight of birds and the sound of a mighty splash. Even Eisenstein would have been proud to do it.'

LEFT
Ollie Junior and Stan Junior having a serious game of checkers in Brats (1930). Using double-exposure and a larger-than-life set, Laurel and Hardy play their own sons, making up the entire cast.

ABOVE
Thelma Todd, visiting the set of Brats, fools around in the gigantic bath. The vivacious Todd appeared five times with the boys, but was best known for starring in comedy shorts opposite Charley Chase. She died aged 30 in mysterious circumstances in 1935.

LEFT
As Stan Laurel and Oliver Hardy were nothing if not big babies as adults, a logical conclusion was reached when trick photography enabled them to play children in Brats, though their characterisations scarcely differed from their grown-up personae. After all, Ollie's nickname was Babe. The child-like duo played dual roles again in Twice Two (1933) and Our Relations (1936).

Below Zero saw the duo down on their luck again, busking on a freezing winter's day in front of an institute for the deaf and dumb! After they move on, a formidable lady passer-by smashes Ollie's double-bass over his head, and throw's Stan's harmonium into the roadway to be crushed by a truck.

During 1930, while making their profitable shorts, (which were often billed bigger than the features they supported), Stan and Ollie provided the comic relief in *The Rogue Song*, a Technicolor musical starring Metropolitan Opera baritone Lawrence Tibbett and directed by Lionel Barrymore. Cast as two Arabs, Ali-Bek and Murza-Bek, they find themselves in a dark cave. Both are curious to know where the other has acquired a fur coat, until they discover they are in a bear's den.

Although they had made brief appearances in a few features, there was still no thought of their making one

themselves. Roach did, however, begin to put them in three and four-reelers, proving that their comedy could be sustained over greater length. The 'old dark house' comedy, *The Laurel and Hardy Murder Case*, a three-reeler, opens with Ollie reading an item in the newspaper about a $3 million will which he thinks they could get hold of. Stan asks, '$3 million! Is that as much as a thousand?' Ollie sighs. 'Why, man alive, it's twice as much!'

Another Fine Mess has them on the run and taking refuge in a house whose owner (James Finlayson) has gone abroad. When a rich couple arrive to rent the place, Ollie pretends to be the owner and Stan doubles as butler and maid. Naturally, the real owner arrives back unexpectedly, and chaos ensues.

The longer three-reel format continued with *Be Big* (1931). This revolves around Stan's attempts to help

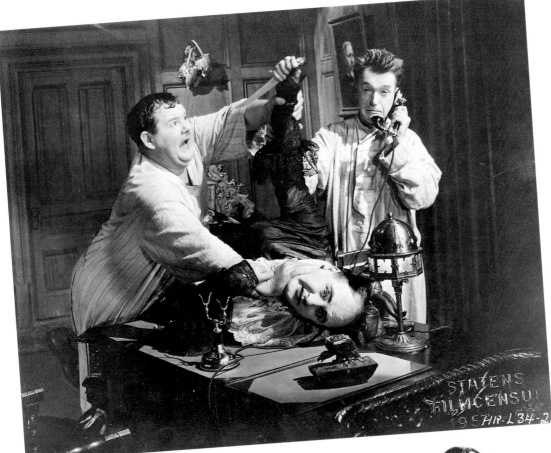

FAR LEFT
As unsuccessful buskers in Below Zero *(1930), when Ollie and Stan are asked by a lady how much they expect to earn per street, ('50 cents'), she chucks them a dollar and asks them to move on two blocks.*

LEFT
Heirs to a fortune, the boys find a corpse in The Laurel and Hardy Murder Case *(1930), their longest short to date running about thirty minutes. The ending of this spoof of Paul Leni's 1927 silent,* The Cat and the Canary, *reveals that the boys had been dreaming the whole thing.*

BELOW
Ollie spends most of Be Big *(1931) trying to rid himself of a pair of Stan's riding boots. To avoid an outing with their wives, Ollie has feigned illness, and Stan has to stay to look after his friend.*

Ollie take off a pair of riding boots which are far too tight for him. The struggle to remove them causes considerable damage to the house, much to the anger of their wives when they return from an outing.

In *Helpmates* (1932), Ollie has taken advantage of his wife's absence to throw a party and Stan comes over to 'help' him clear up the mess before she returns. What follows is an absurd crescendo of destruction which ends with the whole house burning down. 'Well, I guess there's nothing else I can do,' states Stan. 'No, I guess not,' Ollie replies, sitting in the rubble. 'Well, I'll be seeing you,' says Stan hopefully. 'Goodbye,' Ollie murmurs. 'Hey! Would you mind closing the door? I'd like to be alone.' Suddenly, it starts to rain on the roofless house. Ollie philosophically flicks a speck of dust off his trousers, stares at the camera and sighs.

A slow but inexorable build-up to disaster appeared again in *The Music Box*. A virtual remake of *Hats Off* (1927), it uses the same endless flight of steps (in five years the surrounding neighbourhood has been built up) but this time the item the boys are asked to deliver is a large piano in a packing case. Among the obstacles they encounter on their arduous way up to the house is a

maid pushing a pram. Because Ollie gallantly gives her the right of way, the crate breaks loose and bounces down to the bottom of the steps. Stan can't resist kicking the maid's behind. She reports it to a policeman, saying, 'He kicked me in the middle of my daily duties.' They are also impeded by a top-hatted gentleman (Billy Gilbert) who asks the 'two numskulls' to make way for him. When Ollie asks why he doesn't just walk around the box, he replies, 'What? Walk around? Me? Professor Theodore von Schwarzenhoffen, M.D., A.D., D.D.S., F.L.D., F.F.F. und F. should walk around?' When they finally reach the door of the house, they relax hold of the piano and it goes tumbling down to the bottom of the steps again. They eventually arrive back at the top where they meet a postman (Charlie Hall) who says, 'Did you fellows carry that piano all the way up these stairs? You didn't have to do that. Do you see that road down there? All you had to do was to drive around that road to the top here. Whew!' So naturally they take the crate down again and load it on the cart with even more problems ahead of them. The movie, which has become one of their most famous shorts, won the Oscar as best

Live Action Comedy Short Subject. Stan thought it the best picture they ever made. *The Music Box*, like many of their other shorts, was shot in only a few days and in sequence, which probably contributed to their extra impetus. Stan believed that it was not possible to film their kind of slapstick comedy by the normal method of discontinuous shooting.

By 1932, Stan and Ollie had been working feverishly for five years and felt they needed a vacation. They decided to take a trip to Europe together, Stan in order to visit his relatives, and Ollie (with Myrtle in tow) to enjoy the golf courses of Scotland. But when they arrived in Southampton on the *SS Aquitania*, there were crowds to greet them on the dockside, and a band played 'The Cuckoo Song'. Stan was thrilled when his father, Arthur J. Jefferson, and his stepmother came on board to meet them. During their stay in London, they went to see Noel Coward's *Cavalcade* at Drury Lane and took bows standing in the Royal Box. In Glasgow, thirty people were injured in the crush to catch a glimpse of the pair and in Paris, where they are known as 'Laurelardee', they were driven through the thronged

LEFT
When his wife phones to inform him of her return, Ollie's house is now spotless after a spiralling series of catastrophes have taken place, in Helpmates (1932). These included the collapse of a stove pipe, hence the soot, an exploding gas stove, and the toppling over of a pile of dishes. When Ollie has left, Stan decides to light a fire with kerosene!

LEFT
*'La Grande Nuit de Paris
and Stan Laurel welcome
Olivier [sic] Hardy,' reads
the sign. In Paris, the boys'
French fan club greets
Ollie in Stan masks, an
example of the duo's
popularity in France,
where they are known by
the singular soubriquet of
'Laurelardee'. In the pre-
war days, they were at the
height of their inter-
national fame.*

ABOVE
*Stan and Ollie finally
reach the house on the
steep hill after hauling the
piano in a packing case up
an endless flight of steps
in the Oscar-winning* The
Music Box *(1932).
Although it used sound to
enhance the sight gags,
and the boys do a splendid
little dance to the pianola,
the film was rooted in the
great tradition of silent
screen comedy.*

streets in the President's car. They knew that they were
popular, but had never dreamed how well loved they
were outside the States. When they returned to Hollywood they decided to make fewer films. The days of the
comedy short were drawing to an end and they were
forced, against their wishes, to think in terms of making
features.

7
MORE NICE MESSES

'We should have stayed in the short-film category,' Stan stated. 'There is just so much comedy we can do along a certain line and then it gets to be unfunny. You've got to settle for a simple basic story in our case and then work out all the comedy that's there – and then let it alone. But you can't take a long series of things we do and stick them all together in eight reels, and expect to get a well-balanced picture out of it. We didn't want to go into feature films in the first place, and even though I've got some favourites among them, I'm sorry we ever did go beyond the two- and three-reelers.'

Many critics and picturegoers would echo Stan's doubts about the features, but unless Laurel and Hardy had retired from the movies in the thirties (heaven forefend!), the changeover was inevitable. Many of the longer films, never very much over an hour, contained some of their best work. It was only later, after the boys had left Hal Roach and lost a great deal of independence, that the strain began to show.

They had already embarked on a feature film in 1931, the year before their European trip. *Pardon Us* (UK: *Jailbirds*) was originally conceived as a two-reel take-off of *The Big House*, a popular prison movie starring Wallace Beery and Chester Morris, but the set proved so costly that Roach felt he would get more money back on the picture if it were extended by four more reels.

In it, Stan and Ollie are sent to prison for bootlegging. They share a cell with the most intimidating and fearsome inmate of the prison, Tiger (Walter Long), and they attend education classes run by none other than James Finlayson. 'Spell "needle",' Fin asks Ollie. 'N-e-i-d-l-e.' 'There's no 'i' in needle,' explodes the teacher. 'Then, it's a rotten needle,' says Stan. Soon they make their escape, finding themselves in the cotton fields. In order to remain undetected, they black up and join the cotton pickers, with whom Ollie sings 'Lazy Moon' in a pleasant tenor voice, while Stan does an eccentric slide dance. After they are recaptured, the boys unwittingly foil a huge escape and gain pardons. Although most of the fifty-six-minute movie was funny, it did give the impression that there was some padding, especially in the cotton-pickin' sequence.

Beau Hunks (UK: *Beau Chumps*), released a few months after *Pardon Us*, was shorter, being only four reels. It opens with Ollie preparing to get married. 'Who to?' asks Stan. 'Why, a woman of course,' replies Ollie. 'Did you ever hear of anybody marrying a man?' 'Sure,' says Stan. 'My sister.' When Ollie is jilted by her (we see a picture of Jean Harlow), he decides to join the Foreign Legion to forget. Rather reluctantly Stan goes along too. When they get to the desert, they discover

that most of the legionnaires are mooning over the same girl. In the end, after they get lost in the desert, the boys capture the chief of the Riffs, who also happens to have a photo of Jean Harlow in his possession. It's signed: 'To my Sheikie Weekie, from Jeanie Weenie.' Incidentally, the chief was played by the film's director, James W. Horne, under the name of Abdul Kasim K'Horne.

OVERLEAF
Stan and Ollie as bootleggers in stir with a gang of tough cons led by Walter Long (prisoner 31752) in Pardon Us (1931), Laurel and Hardy's first feature-length (56 minutes) movie. Their films were to get longer, though not necessarily better.

ABOVE
Stan Laurel and Oliver Hardy are captured by the Riffs in Beau Hunks known as Beau Chumps in Great Britain.

FAR LEFT
The boys being in prison for bootlegging in Pardon Us failed to alienate American audiences, most of whom believed that Prohibition was there to be broken anyway.

LEFT
A publicity still for Beau Hunks (1931), a forty-minute feature, in which the duo joins the Foreign Legion.

In *Pack up your Troubles* (1932), their longest film yet at sixty-eight minutes, Stan and Ollie are recruited into the army during World War I. There they are faced by a brutal drill sergeant (Frank Brownlee) and a choleric general (James Finlayson). At the end of hostilities, they go in search of the grandparents of the little daughter of Eddie Smith, their buddy who was killed in the war. The problem is, the only information they have is that the relatives are called Smith!

Although Laurel and Hardy shorts were still being produced, fewer and fewer were made from 1933; yet their first features were merely extensions of the sort of things they had done in the short form. Gradually, Roach put them into screenplays in which they became an integral part of a more intricate plot including romance and musical numbers. As Stanlio and Ollio, they appeared for the first time in period costume and wigs in the MGM feature *Fra Diavolo* (aka *The Devil's Brother*). This was based on Auber's comic opera about a bandit in 18th-century Italy. When the pair's life savings are stolen the best way to recoup their losses is to become bandits themselves. One of the first people they hold-up is Fra Diavolo (Dennis King) whom Ollie pretends to be. The real bandit then uses the boys in a

plot to rob Lord and Lady Rocberg (James Finlayson and Thelma Todd). Hal Roach himself directed most of the picture, with Charley Rogers (who was to direct seven Laurel and Hardy movies) directing the boys' sequences – one of the best being a game called 'kneesie-earsie-nosie'. This requires the player to slap both knees, pull the nose with the left hand while simultaneously pulling the left ear with the right hand, and then switch hands and ears. Audiences could be seen leaving the theatre attempting to emulate Stan's expertise at the game.

LEFT
Stan and Ollie asleep on guard as First World War army rookies in Pack up your Troubles *(1932)*. Naturally, the army is at war with them. This, their second full-length feature, was co-directed by Ray McCarey, Leo McCarey's 28-year-old younger brother, who died aged 44.

RIGHT AND ABOVE
Pack up your Troubles departed from many of Laurel and Hardy's earlier films by having a stronger story line – not just a succession of gags – as well as a heart-tugging sequence with four-year-old Jacquie Lyn from London whom Hal Roach signed for 'Our Gang' shorts.

Their next feature, *Sons of the Desert* (UK: *Fraternally Yours*), one of their best, was among the ten top-grossing films of 1934. Using the old theme of husbands trying to escape wives, it reached new and very funny heights of absurdity. Stan and Ollie are members of a fez-wearing fraternity that excludes women, so when they're invited to the convention in Chicago they seem to have a problem. 'Do you have to ask your wife everything?' says Ollie. 'Well, if I didn't ask her, I wouldn't know what she wanted me to do.' 'I go places . . . and then tell my wife. Every man should be the king in his own castle.' But Mrs Hardy (Mae Busch) has other ideas. The two errant husbands concoct a scheme that will convince their wives that Ollie needs a cruise to Honolulu because of his health, and then go off to the convention in Chicago.

At the convention they have a great time drinking, dancing, singing 'Honolulu Baby', playing practical jokes on the other Sons and having them played on them, mainly by Charley Chase (a favourite comedian and director in the twenties). Unfortunately, the ship on which they were supposed to be cruising sinks, and their wives go down to the steamship company to hear the details. To take their minds off the possible demise of their spouses, the girls go to a movie theatre where they see a newsreel of the convention which shows their cavorting husbands clearly. Needless to say, Stan and

Ollie get it in the neck from their wives when they return home.

Sons of the Desert is a Laurel and Hardy favourite among adult fans, but the pair's greatest appeal has always been to children, who find it easy to identify with these two kids in adult form. Conscious of this, Roach produced one of the few musicals aimed specifically at children. Stannie Dum and Ollie Dee are toymakers in *Babes in Toyland* (1934), which was adapted

ABOVE
At the boys' fez-wearing fraternity known as the Sons of the Desert, Charley Chase (second left) plays an unappreciated practical joke on another member.

BELOW
Stannie Dum and Ollie Dee find themselves in the stocks in Babes In Toyland *(1934).*

BOTTOM
Babes in Toyland *was one of the few musicals intentionally aimed at children.*

RIGHT
Babes In Toyland, *a perennial favourite with kids and adults, is frequently screened on American TV at Christmas.*

from the Victor Herbert musical comedy. Due to their characteristic ineptitude, instead of making six hundred toy soldiers one foot high, they make one hundred soldiers six foot high. When the city's ramparts are stormed by baddies in the shape of furry Bogeymen, they are defeated by the combined efforts of Stan and Ollie, the giant toy soldiers, and other characters in Toyland, including Little Boy Blue, Mother Goose, and even Santa Claus. It was all rather like the kind of English pantomime Stan had seen in his youth.

In between the features, they still made the odd two-reeler in which they felt happiest. One of the better ones was *The Fixer Uppers* (1935), in which the boys play Christmas-card salesmen, with verses written by Stan such as, 'Jingle bells, jingle bells, coming through the rye, I wish you a merry Xmas, even as you and I', and 'Merry Christmas, mother. Merry Christmas, ma. Hi, mommy, mommy – and a hot cha cha!'

Meanwhile, both Stan and Ollie were having marital problems. In 1930, Stan and Lois suffered a severe blow

with the death of their son, Stanley Robert, who was born prematurely and lived a mere nine days. Stan was involved in affairs before the eventual divorce from Lois, and continued to have them even after he met and married Virginia Ruth Rogers in 1934, especially with Alyce Ardell, his long-time girlfriend. It is therefore not surprising that Stan's second marriage petered out after a couple of years. Ollie and Myrtle separated in 1935 and were divorced in 1937.

In 1935, Stan and Ollie went back to making feature films with *Bonnie Scotland*, a partial pastiche of *Lives of a Bengal Lancer*, released just a few months before. It

LEFT
Kilted Stan and Ollie, *bayonets at the ready, in* **Bonnie Scotland** *(1935), far more dangerous to their friends than to their enemies.*

ABOVE
Babes in Toyland, *with its tuneful Victor Herbert score, was released under different titles. This poster is for* **March of the Wooden Soldiers.**

STAN
LAUREL
OLIVER
HARDY
THE BOHEMIAN GIRL
It's A FULL LENGTH ATOMIComedy   PRODUCED BY HAL ROACH
Released thru FILM CLASSICS Inc.

proved to be their biggest world-wide box-office hit so far. Stan, of course, got a larger salary than Ollie, because he contributed more to the creative process. He plays Stan McLaurel, who inherits part of his Scottish grandfather's estate, a snuffbox and a set of bagpipes. The second half of the film shows the boys as part of a Scottish regiment in India, where they are the bane of sergeant James Finlayson, whom they refer to as 'Sergeant Leatherpuss'. Among the highlights are Stan's grilling a fish on a candle under a hotel bed, and his getting the entire regiment to march in his (wrong) step.

In the same year, Hal Roach, recalling the critical and

ABOVE
Thelma Todd in The Bohemian Girl, *her last screen appearance before her premature death during the shooting. Todd, originally cast as the heroine, sings one song (dubbed).*

TOP LEFT
Any resemblance between The Bohemian Girl *and Michael W. Balfe's renowned operetta of the same name was purely coincidental, but it did have a fair share of the original score.*

LEFT
Laurel and Hardy play a pair of Gypsy rogues in The Bohemian Girl *(1936). Here, Stan gets to kiss Mae Busch under Ollie's disapproving eyes.*

commercial success of *Fra Diavolo*, returned the duo to the world of operetta with Michael Balfe's *The Bohemian Girl*, which included the song 'I Dreamt I Dwelt in Marble Halls'. In between the numbers, Stan and Ollie were given plenty of scope for comedy as a pair of Gypsy rogues who adopt a little girl unaware that she is a princess. One of the best routines was Stan gradually getting drunk while bottling wine, a variation of the flagon-drinking gag in *Fra Diavalo*.

Sadly, soon after shooting, Thelma Todd, the lovely blonde comedienne, was found dead of carbon monoxide poisoning in her parked car. She was thirty years old. Nobody has ever discovered whether it was suicide, murder or an accident. She was much loved on the Roach lot, and her loss was keenly felt by Laurel and Hardy, with whom she had made five pictures.

The Bohemian Girl was the seventh full-length feature the boys had made for Roach, not to mention sixty-four shorts, and their relationship was beginning to show some signs of strain. Stan wanted more control over future productions and battled to persuade Roach to draw up a new contract. They did manage to squeeze a little more independence from Roach, and slightly better financial benefit from their next two pictures under the banner of Stan Laurel Productions. The films, in fact, turned out to be two of their best.

In *Our Relations* (1936) Stan and Ollie play themselves and their twin brothers, Alfie Laurel and Bert Hardy, causing double trouble when they turn up at different times at Denkers's Beer Garden. It would be impossible to describe the twists and turns of the comedy of errors, except to say that among those confused were James Finlayson, Alan Hale, and Iris Adrian who liked to deliver her lines at the top of her voice.

TOP
Stan and Ollie play happily married men (seen here with their wives Betty Healy and Daphne Pollard) in Our Relations **(1936), whose lives are disrupted by their twin sailor brothers.**

LEFT
Complications ensue when Stan and Ollie, as well as Alfie Laurel and Bert Hardy arrive at Denker's Beer Garden in Our Relations, **and meet the sailor boys' shipmate James Finlayson.**

Way Out West (1937) was even funnier, yet it is the musical number that Stan and Ollie perform inside and outside a saloon bar that most audiences remember with affection. They do an elegantly eccentric dance outside the saloon, while cowboys sing, followed by Ollie and Stan's harmonizing in 'The Trail of the Lonesome Pine'. Stan's delightful tenor voice alters to a deep base (provided by Chill Wills) and suddenly changes again into a high soprano (Rosina Lawrence) when Ollie bops him on the head with a mallet. At the climax, the pair sing 'We're Going to Go Way Down in Dixie'. The plot involved Stan and Ollie in the town of Brushwood Gulch. The boy's mission is to give the title deeds of a goldmine to Mary Roberts (Rosina Lawrence) whose

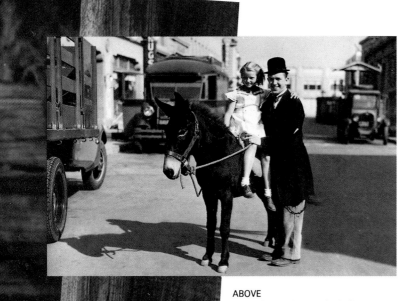

ABOVE
Lois Laurel, aged eight, enjoying a ride on Dinah the Donkey on the Hal Roach backlot during the filming of Way Out West. *At this time, Stan was divorced from Lois's mother.*

LEFT
Laurel and Hardy with Dinah the Donkey in Way Out West *(1936), their last comic masterpiece. It was also the last of a dozen of Laurel and Hardy films directed by James W. Horne.*

RIGHT
Although there were brilliantly timed comic routines in Way Out West, *it is the two musical numbers that most people remember. It is often forgotten that both Stan and Ollie had very pleasant singing voices.*

dead father was their buddy. The bartender of the saloon (James Finlayson) tries to do her out of the deeds.

In the same year, the boys guest-starred in a musical called *Pick a Star*, in which Rosina Lawrence comes to Hollywood to be discovered, and sees Laurel and Hardy at the studios. In the first of their two appearances, they play Mexican bandits with false moustaches in a saloon where Ollie keeps getting hit on the head with a bottle meant for Stan. Sitting in the director's chair is a clean-shaven Finlayson. They crop up again in a sequence during which Ollie swallows a mouth organ and Stan plays a tune by pressing his ample stomach.

In contrast, Stan and Ollie next found themselves in *Swiss Miss* (1938) as itinerant mousetrap salesmen in a Hollywood-style Switzerland – the most logical place to be, because it is the country of cheese. Not having made a single sale in the two weeks since their arrival, the pair wind up as waiters at a hotel where they display their usual maladroitness. The action takes place during a music festival, and everybody goes around singing and dancing, while Stan and Ollie try to help out a famous composer who is having problems with his wife and his new operetta.

One of the best gags has Stan plucking chickens

LEFT
An overhead shot of a sound stage at the Hal Roach studios during the filming of Way Out West. *The fact that this sixty-six minute movie, one of Laurel and Hardy's biggest successes, was produced by Stan, who had a great deal of control, proved his creative genius. He was never to have such power again, and the later films were never as good.*

outside the hotel kitchen, and trying to persuade a St Bernard dog to let him have a swig from the brandy flask hung about its thick neck. He does this by pretending to be a man trapped in a snowstorm by throwing the feathers into the air. The most hilarious comedy sequence, reminiscent of *The Music Box*, is when Stan and Ollie have to carry a piano up to the composer's tree-house high in the mountains. Along the way they cross a swaying rope-bridge, suspended a thousand feet above a Swiss gorge, and meet a gorilla coming the other way! Although James Agee thought it one of the genuinely great moments in film comedy, it might have been even funnier had the studio not

ABOVE
Laurel and Hardy seem to be enjoying themselves on the set of Swiss Miss (1938) with the make-up girl. Stan's normally white clown's face usually didn't require much make-up, but 46-year-old Ollie continually needed his hair and tooth-brush moustache darkening.

RIGHT
Oliver Hardy on his way to the shops to buy a present for his wife with the dollar he has had to borrow from her, comes across one of his high-hatted neigh-bours in Block-Heads (1938). Later in the movie, Ollie has to walk the thirteen floors up when the elevator is out of order.

interfered with the final edited version. Originally the piano contained a bomb which would be triggered off when a certain key was struck. Losing the bomb in the cutting destroyed the suspense when the inebriated Stan kept hitting the keyboard.

Nothing in *Block-Heads* (1938) topped the film's opening gag. It begins with the boys in the trenches during World War I, and then cuts to twenty years later with Stan still standing guard. Nobody told him the war was over! The camera pans slowly to reveal a mountain of the empty cans of beans he has consumed in that time. When he is finally relieved of his post and Ollie takes him home, it seems Stan has not changed at all, and the two of them wreck the kitchen in a gas explosion.

Meanwhile, the duo's disagreements with Hal Roach

were increasing, and it was rumoured that *Block-Heads* would be the last Laurel and Hardy movie for his production company. In the event, it was their last Roach film to be released by MGM, but there were still two more films to make with the producer before their decline set in.

ABOVE
After being away from America for twenty years at war, Stan manages to wreck Ollie's car and garage in Block-Heads, having missed the special plate that opens the doors automatically.

BABES IN HOLLYWOOD

8

Not only were there rumours that Laurel and Hardy were leaving Hal Roach, but it was said they were leaving each other. Why was Ollie making a film without Stan? Had the friends fallen out? Was there jealousy and rivalry between them? Absolutely not. Actually, Stan and Ollie had separate contracts with Roach, each terminating at a different time, Stan's in 1939 and Ollie's a year later. Stan decided to wait until his partner was free before negotiating another joint contract for them.

Without Laurel, Hardy was united with Harry Langdon, the faded baby-faced silent movie comedian, in *Zenobia* (GB: *Elephants Never Forget*, 1939). In order to avoid comparison with the famous partnership, the screenwriters got Langdon and Hardy to play two separate characters among many in a cast that included Billie Burke, Alice Brady, Stepin Fetchit and Hattie McDaniel. The somewhat lumbering comedy took place in a small Southern town in 1870, where Professor Langdon goes to Doctor Hardy to have a knot untied from the tail of his elephant. Thereafter, the beast follows Hardy about like a faithful dog, and Langdon sues the doctor for alienation of affection. The public could have sued Mr Roach for the same reason, but the movie did give Ollie a chance to try playing a role that differed from his usual one. Thankfully, Laurel and Hardy were back together again soon after.

Taking advantage of their temporary release from Roach, Stan and Ollie moved over to RKO for their next picture, *The Flying Deuces* (1939). The boys starred as two Iowan fishmongers in Paris, where Ollie's marriage proposal has been turned down by the woman he loves. He contemplates suicide, trying to persuade Stan to do the same, but when Stan refuses to follow his friend to the death, the two of them enlist in the French Foreign Legion, and spend the rest of the film trying to get out. They finally escape in a pilotless airplane. In one delightful sequence, Ollie sings 'Shine On Harvest Moon', while Stan does a brief soft shoe dance. The film, co-written by Harry Langdon, was a hit, and led to RKO's upgrading the level of comedy on its schedules. *The Flying Deuces* was also important personally for Ollie, because on it he met Lucille Jones, the continuity girl with whom he was to live for the rest of his life.

Ollie was divorced from Myrtle, and was contemplating marrying Viola Morse, his girlfriend of many years, when he met and married Lucille in 1940. Stan was less lucky in love. He had divorced Ruth in January 1938 to marry Vera Ivanova Shuvalova, a Russian-born singer and dancer known professionally as Illeana, who claimed to be a countess. At the same time, the gossip columns were full of reports that his former lover, Mae Dahlberg, had returned from Australia to demand money from him. In fact, they met briefly and she didn't ask him for a penny. He would not have been able to give her much anyway.

Although Stan did not want to sign another contract with Roach because he was hoping to get a better deal and more independence for Ollie and himself, he urgently needed money to sort out his various marital

OVERLEAF
Stan and Ollie as two convicts on the run in Liberty (1929), who somehow find themselves high up on a construction site, when Ollie discovers that a crab has sidled into his pants at the fish market.

LEFT
During the one-picture separation from Stan, Ollie teamed up unsuccessfully with Harry Langdon in Zenobia (1939).

RIGHT
The role of Doctor Henry Tebbitt in Zenobia gave Oliver Hardy the opportunity to play a semi-straight comic part, which he had always hankered to do. It would be another ten years until another chance in The Fighting Kentuckian, also without Stan.

difficulties. The team, therefore, reluctantly agreed to do four films for Roach, who knew the boys were still big at the box office. Actually, it was associate producer, twenty-year-old Hal Roach Jr with whom they had to deal on the lot.

'We never had no education. We're not illiterate enough,' says Stan in *A Chump at Oxford* (1940), Roach's slapstick answer to MGM's *A Yank at Oxford*, starring Robert Taylor. In this case, Stan and Ollie were rewarded with an Oxford education by a grateful

banker after they had inadvertently captured a bank robber. Things moved even further from the realms of the possible when the two of them turned up at an unlikely college wearing Eton suits and mortar boards. When it's pointed out that they're dressed for Eton, Stan says, 'Well, that's swell. We haven't eaten since breakfast.' At Oxford, they are remorselessly ragged by the elderly-looking students, one of whom is Peter Cushing (in his second film). Just as Ollie had an opportunity to stray from his habitual screen character in *Zenobia*, Stan was permitted, due to a twist in the plot, co-devised by Harry Langdon, to play the complete opposite to his usual dunderhead. An accidental blow on the head transforms Stan into Lord Paddington, the college's greatest athlete and scholar, who had suffered amnesia and left for the USA, a complete idiot. Now restored to his true self, Paddington rules the roost and employs Ollie, whom he refers to as 'Fatty, old thing', as his manservant. Needless to say, another blow on the head brings back the cowardly and brainless Stan we love, much to Ollie's relief.

There was a good quota of inspired moments in *Saps at Sea* (also 1940), half of which was taken up with Stan and Ollie doing their saps-on-land routine. This included a scene in which the handiwork of a plumber (played by cross-eyed Ben Turpin) causes a fridge to play music and a radio to produce ice. Ollie works in a horn factory and goes berserk because of the constant hooting, so Dr James Finlayson (in the last of his thirty-three films with them) advises a sea voyage to remedy Ollie's acute case of 'hornophobia'. But the boys are shanghaied by an escaped murderer (Dick Cramer), who gets them to eat a meal (meant for him) made up of wax, talcum, tobacco and twine in the form of bacon, biscuits and spaghetti.

Saps at Sea ended Laurel and Hardy's thirteen-year

BELOW
Not exactly Einsteins, undergraduates Laurel and Hardy have difficulty coping with the simplest problems in A Chump at Oxford.

RIGHT
In Saps at Sea (1940), Stan drives Ollie mad in the horn-making factory, the film that ended their 13-year partnership with Hal Roach.

association with Hal Roach, and the boys faced the future full of renewed vigour and enthusiasm. In their private lives, Stan's marriage to Illeana had quickly burnt itself out. They divorced in 1940, and he was preparing to remarry Ruth, his former second wife, a year later. Ollie had settled down happily with Lucille.

Before embarking on another film, they satisfied their longing to play before live audiences again in *The Laurel and Hardy Revue*, a show that included a chorus line, variety acts and a thirty-minute sketch by the stars. The revue enjoyed a successful tour of the Midwest and East, entertained troops in the Caribbean, and returned to play Chicago and Detroit before Ollie's laryngitis forced them to close prior to their planned engagement in Boston.

Putting their minds back to film, they formed their own company, Laurel and Hardy Feature Productions, finally realising Stan's dream. But the dream soon turned to nightmare, and the company never made a film. They lacked the vast amount of capital needed for

RIGHT
Laurel and Hardy being misled by a gangster's crony posing as a widow in A-Haunting We Will Go *(1942), in order to transport a coffin by train from Los Angeles to Dayton Ohio. The casket, in fact, doesn't contain a corpse, but the gangster himself.*

RIGHT
**A-Haunting We Will Go,
was a slight improvement
on** Great Guns **(1941),
Laurel and Hardy's first
film for Twentieth
Century-Fox. None of the
old team were involved in
it, though Margaret Roach,
Hal's daughter, had a
small role, billed as Diana
Rochelle.**

hiring studios and technicians, as well as the means of
distribution, and they were forced once again to make
movies for one of the major studios. Full of great
expectations, Stan and Ollie joined Twentieth Century-
Fox in 1941. Although profits shot up in the early
forties due to the wartime growth in filmgoing, Fox
was cutting down their expenditure on B pictures,
which included those of Laurel and Hardy. On the very
first day the duo arrived at Fox for *Great Guns*, they
realised they would be nothing more than employees
with most of their creative input stifled at birth. As a
result, the film shows them as pale shadows of their
former selves, with only a few moments to remind
audiences of the Roach days.

In *Great Guns*, Stan and Ollie were cast as the
chauffeur and gardener to a millionaire's son. When
their employer is drafted, the pair join up in order to
look after him in the Army. (There's no point in
wondering how anyone of Ollie's age and weight could
have passed the physical.) Of course, they come into
conflict with Sergeant Hippo (Edward MacDonald trying to imitate Edgar Kennedy's slow burns), mainly
because they insisted on bringing along their pet crow,
Penelope. The leaden comedy was the first (and last)
American film to be directed by the Italian-born Monty
Banks (Mario Bianchi), the husband of Gracie Fields,
who had made a career in England.

Their second film for Fox, *A-Haunting We Will Go*
(1942) was no better, although it started promisingly by
offering a familiar glimpse of Stan and Ollie down on

their luck and looking for a job. Eventually, they are hired to deliver a coffin by train, but complications arise when the coffin gets accidentally switched with a magician's trunk.

Temporarily free from Fox, their next movie, *Air Raid Wardens* (1943), was a return to MGM, the scene of earlier triumphs. It was also good to have Edgar Kennedy, a survivor from their stock company, in the cast as an irate removal man. Although some smiles were engendered in the over-plotted tale of Stan and Ollie's foiling an attempt to sabotage a chemical plant, much of the potential fun was dampened by a Civil Defence directive stating that the job of the wardens must in no way be ridiculed. Not easy to make a comedy under those conditions.

Back at Fox, *Jitterbugs* (1943) showed a slight improvement, because the plot gave the boys more leeway, especially the scenes with Stan disguised as a rich aunt

and Ollie as a Southern gentleman (which he liked to think of himself as in reality). Also in it was the twenty-one-year-old blonde singer called Vivian Blaine, who would later make a hit on Broadway and on film in *Guys and Dolls*. Stan appeared again in drag in *The Dancing Masters* of the same year, this time in a ballerina's costume. An early appearance by the young Robert Mitchum as a hood, and the presence of Margaret Dumont, the Marx Brothers' great foil, lent some interest to the tired proceedings. As for *The Big Noise* (1944), according to one critic, 'it can be put into a sentence: the boys had to deliver a powerful bomb.

RIGHT
Stan and Ollie play the title roles in The Dancing Masters *(1943), running the Arthur Hurry School of Dancing. It necessitated Stan's dressing up in a tutu as a dancing mistress.*

LEFT
For the purposes of the plot of Jitterbugs (1943), Oliver Hardy pretends to be 'Colonel' Wetterson Boxby, a philandering Texan and Stan Laurel a Bostonian dowager called Aunt Emily.

RIGHT
Stan and Ollie struggling to be funny while doing their bit for the war effort in Air Raid Wardens (1943), in face of the Civil Defence directive that the wartime role of the air warden must not be ridiculed.

Laurel and Hardy as incompetent detectives, despite Stan's deerstalker and pipe, in The Big Noise *(1944). They are hired by an inventor to guard an explosive device, but they didn't reckon on his crazy sleep-walking sister-in-law (Doris Merrick).*

Stan Laurel is mistaken for his double, none other than the famous matador Don Sebastian, in The Bullfighters *(1945), the last of the boys' feeble Twentieth Century-Fox movies. It was the strongest evidence yet how much Stan and Ollie were showing their age. A rival bullfighter was played by up-and-coming Rory Calhoun.*

Forced to go into the bull ring in The Bullfighters, *Stan goes into his celebrated crying routine for the umpteenth and penultimate time on screen. Ollie, in sombrero, still manages to put a brave face on it.*

They did.' The best moment was the revival of their old two-men-in-a-berth routine from *Berth Marks* of 1929. Unfortunately, Stan's request to update it by setting the sequence in a plane flying through a storm rather than a train was flatly turned down by Fox executives. Another link with the past was Eddie Dearing, who played the motorcycle cop, the same role he had had sixteen years previously in *Two Tars*.

Stan and Ollie's last picture for Fox hit a further low. It was rather sad to see fifty-five-year-old Stan and fifty-three-year-old Ollie frantically scrabbling for laughs in *The Bullfighters* (1945). The plot had them sent to Mexico as private detectives; inevitably Stan is mistaken for a famous Spanish matador and has to substitute in the ring for the real one. The fight itself is cut in with footage from the Tyrone Power remake of *Blood and Sand*, of a few years before. The last four of their Fox films were all directed by Malcolm St Clair, who had himself seen better days. He had been best known previously for directing a few sophisticated silents such as *Gentlemen Prefer Blondes*, and jazz-age musicals.

But the torture for Laurel and Hardy fans was not over yet. There was still one more movie for MGM to prolong the agony. At least *Nothing But Trouble* (1945)

looked as though a little more money had been spent on it, and it had its moments (literally). In it, Stan and Ollie are butler and chef to a wealthy family who have invited King Christopher of Orlandia, a boy monarch in exile, to dinner, not knowing that his life is in danger from his wicked uncle Prince Saul. Naturally, the boys saved the day, but not the picture. It marked the one-off return to films of director Sam Taylor after ten years as a publicist. He was infamous for the credit on the Pickford-Fairbanks *Taming of the Shrew* – 'by William Shakespeare; additional dialogue by Sam Taylor'.

It seemed it was time for Stan and Ollie to call it a day. 'What was there for us to do but get out?' remarked Stan. 'We had no say in those films, and it sure looked it. We had done too many films in our own way for us to keep taking anything like that, so we gave up the ghost. It was sickening.'

In compensation, Stan had found a woman to whom he would stay married for the rest of his life. She was Ida Kitaeva Raphael, a singer born in China of White Russian parents. They married in 1946. Despite the marked decline in their films during the last five years, there was still great affection for them worldwide, as they were soon to find out.

RIGHT
Oliver Hardy, Stan and Ida Laurel choosing a pair of braces at Simpson's, Piccadilly during the duos 1947–48 tour of the English music halls. It was a pleasant escape from the unsatisfying grind of their last films.

LEAVE 'EM LAUGHING

9

Considering their film careers over, but still wanting to work, Stan and Ollie jumped at the chance when they were invited by British impresario, Bernard Delfont, to tour the English music halls in 1947. Lucille Hardy and Ida Laurel accompanied their husbands on the nine-month tour which culminated at the renowned London Palladium. It was a happy experience for both entertainers. Ollie managed to get in several rounds of golf, and Stan was able to visit his relatives.

His father was living with Stan's sister who ran a pub in Grantham, Lincolnshire. Old A. J. was extremely proud of his famous son, who had come from the English music hall tradition of which he himself had been a part. After a Royal Command Performance, the show went on to Scandinavia, France and Belgium with equal success.

On their return to the USA, Stan paid a visit to Charlie Chaplin, his old colleague from the Fred Karno days, who had just had his first major film flop with *Monsieur Verdoux*. The ostensible reason for the visit was that Stan had been given a book by a Fleet Street journalist inscribed to Chaplin, and he decided to hand it to the great man in person. They spent a very pleasant

OVERLEAF
'One lump, or two?'. Mr Hardy helps his friend Mr Laurel to the sugar.

Charles Chaplin as Monsieur Verdoux (1947), his first film for six years since the success of The Great Dictator. *Both critics and audiences were generally hostile to this 'comedy of murders'. His appearance before the House UnAmerican Activities Committee would alienate him further from the public. He and Stan met for the last time in 1947.*

LEFT
Stan Laurel and Oliver Hardy, with their wives, Ida and Lucille, shopping in Oxford Street during their 1947 tour of Great Britain. Stan had married Ida Kitaeva Raphael the previous year. They would remain married for the rest of his life. Ollie had also settled down happily with Lucille since their marriage in 1941.

day together in Beverly Hills talking of old times, but they never saw one another again.

As for Ollie, he was delighted to accept a solo film role in the Republic Pictures Western, *The Fighting Kentuckian* (1949), starring John Wayne and Vera Ralston. In the role of Willie Payne, Wayne's bumbling side-kick, he provided effective comic relief. The following year, Ollie took the small but telling part of a drunk in Frank Capra's horse-racing comedy-drama, *Riding High*, in a cast headed by Bing Crosby. It seemed as though Ollie would continue as a supporting player, while Stan remained inactive. Was the team of Laurel and Hardy a thing of the past?

Then, out of the blue, came an offer to make another film together. A French production company asked if

BELOW
Oliver Hardy took fourth billing in The Fighting Kentuckian *(1949), below John Wayne (centre), Vera Ralston and Philip Dorn (seated), Ollie not only provides laughs, but helps save Wayne's life at the finale.*

Stan and Ollie would be prepared to spend three months shooting on the French Riviera. How could they refuse? It proved however to be an unfortunate decision, to say the least. The catalogue of disasters began when the two of them arrived in Paris only to learn that the story had not even been written. So Stan and a couple of American writers quickly cobbled together a script which involved the boys being cast away on a coral island in the South Seas, where they discover uranium. Secondly, the French director, Leo Joannon, didn't know what was going on, nor it seems did the mixed French and Italian cast (including Suzy Delair and Luigi Tosi) and crew. (It was a French/Italian co-production). Thirdly, Stan became seriously ill and was rushed to hospital to undergo an operation for the removal of a prostate growth. At the same time, it was discovered that he was a diabetic. As a result, Stan's weight was reduced from 165 lbs to a mere 114. With a medical team permanently on the set in case of a relapse, Stan, weak and in pain, carried on with the shooting. The film, variously titled *Atoll K*, *Robinson Crusoeland* and *Utopia*, instead of taking twelve weeks to make, took twelve months! (From April 1950 to April 1951).

There might have been some compensation for all this if the finished product had displayed even an iota of quality. But the sad truth is that the final Laurel and Hardy movie was also their very worst. Both Stan and Ollie looked tired and old and, in Stan's case, ill. It started out lasting ninety-eight interminable minutes, then was cut in the USA (where it was released three years later) to eighty-two minutes, until it ended up on TV in a half-hour version. What a way to end a great film career! Yet, despite the aberrations of the last few years, the memory of The Thin One and The Fat One at their best was preserved in the hearts of their fans.

By 1952, Stan had recovered sufficiently to take on another nine-month tour of Britain, playing once again to full houses. He was even stronger for a tour the following year. It was when their ship was docked at the port of Cobh in Ireland that a remarkable and heart-warming event took place. When word reached the city that Laurel and Hardy were on board, thousands of people came down to the docks to greet them and the many boats in the harbour started blowing their whistles. Then all the church bells in Cobh began

ringing out 'The Cuckoo Song', their theme tune. 'Babe looked at me and we cried,' recalled Stan. 'Maybe people loved us and our pictures because we put so much love in them. I don't know. I'll never forget that day. Never. It's strange, a strange thing. Our popularity has lasted so long. Our last good pictures were made in the thirties, and you'd think people would forget, but they don't. The love and affection we found that day in Cobh was simply unbelievable.'

They were not forgotten in the States either. Many of the old Laurel and Hardy films had been sold to TV, and they were shown all over America. They were, however, rather badly chopped up to suit TV scheduling, and many of them were even crudely retitled – *Alpine Antics* for *Swiss Miss*, *Wacky Westerners* for *Way Out West* etc. Nevertheless, kids discovered Stan and Ollie at their best for the first time, and adults were delighted to be able to laugh at their antics again. Fan mail began to flood in, and the TV stations received thousands of calls, many of them enquiring whether the duo were still alive. Although it gave them great personal satisfaction, they did not receive a cent from the showings, while others grew rich on their past efforts.

In December 1954, Ralph Edwards surprised them both at the Knickerbocker Hotel in Hollywood for NBC's *This Is Your Life*. They had gone there ostensibly

LAKE LAUREL AND HARDY

SO NAMED
BECAUSE THESE TWO
WORLD FAMOUS COMEDIANS
WERE FIRST TEAMED HERE AT
THE HAL ROACH STUDIOS
AND BECAUSE THEY
MORE THAN ANY OTHERS,
WERE IN AND OUT OF
THESE WATERS

"THIS IS YOUR LIFE"
DECEMBER 1, 1954.

ABOVE
**Hal Roach (right) and Hal
Roach Junior (left) pose
beside the plaque
presented to Laurel and
Hardy by Ralph Edwards on
This Is Your Life.**

to meet Bernard Delfont, who was visiting the USA at the time, when the big red book was shoved in their faces. The live programme was rather embarrassing for all concerned. When they got to the studio from the hotel, Edwards had to ad-lib desperately before the duo made a belated entrance. Apparently, Stan insisted Ollie and he rehearse a bit of business before they went on. As friends, relatives and past acquaintances were being trotted out, Stan said very few words – he resented not having had enough time to prepare for the broadcast, and he hated appearing free – while Ollie seemed confused by the whole affair. However, when Ollie was faced with an old woman claiming to be his childhood sweetheart, of whom he obviously had no recollection, he said gallantly, 'She's still beautiful.'

Following this tribute, and recognising that the boys were still popular, Hal Roach Jr, who had taken over his father's studio, offered Stan and Ollie a contract to make four sixty-minute colour films to be shown on NBC in the 1957–1958 season. The series was to be called *Laurel and Hardy's Fabulous Fables*, and were to be made up of many of the sketches and gags that Stan had never had the chance to use in their movies, as well as some old music hall and English pantomime routines refurbished. The format was to have been that of a fairy story in which the boys would play the Babes in the Wood. What the programmes would have been like must remain in the realm of conjecture; ten days before shooting, Stan had a stroke. Fortunately it was mild,

BELOW
Laurel and Hardy, on their 1947–1948 music-hall tour of Great Britain, take another 'photo opportunity' at Simpson's, Piccadilly.

In 1952, the welcome Stan and Ollie received at Cobh, Ireland brought tears to their eyes. The church bells played 'The Cuckoo Song' and the boys were greeted by thousands of fans. 'The love and affection we found that day in Cobh was simply unbelievable', Stan was to comment.

but it left him with a pronounced limp and he had to take life easy. The TV series was abandoned. Stan had already indicated that he was not happy with the way things were going. He said he could not understand the TV people, and he had no real liking for the new medium.

As Stan was on the road to recovery, Ollie was taken ill with a heart condition. Told to lose weight by his doctor, he managed to get down from twenty stone (300 lbs) to thirteen (185 lbs). Nevertheless, in September 1956, he suffered a stroke that left him incapable of movement or speech. He also had a gall bladder attack but surgery was impossible because of his heart condition. 'His spirits seemed to improve when we brought him home from the hospital, but he got frustrated by his inability to do things,' explained Lucille Hardy. 'He would sit and look at a newspaper and then get irritated because he couldn't absorb it. We put him in a wheel chair one day and brought him into the den to see TV. He was always such an avid watcher. But it was evident he couldn't comprehend what was going on. Sometimes he got so upset over his inability to get better that it seemed he almost wished it was all over with.'

Oliver Hardy died on 7th August, 1957. Stan was forbidden by his doctor to attend the funeral, but Ida Laurel was there to comfort Lucille. 'I was terribly shocked when Babe died,' Stan told John McCabe. 'I had just got through answering hundreds and hundreds of letters of good wishes from old fans all over the world who were praying for him, lighting candles for him. He was like a brother to me. We seemed to sense each other. Funny, we never really got to know each other personally until we took tours together. When we made pictures, it was all business even though it was fun. Between pictures we hardly saw each other. His life outside the studio was sports – and my life was practically all work, even after work was over. I loved editing and cutting the pictures, something he wasn't interested in. But whatever I did was tops with him. There was never any argument between us, ever. I hope wherever he is now that he realizes how much people loved him.'

Stan, who had remained a British citizen, was awarded a special Oscar for 'creative pioneering in the field of cinema comedy' in 1961. He and his wife lived

modestly at the Oceana Apartment Hotel, Oceana Avenue, Santa Monica, where he often received visits from admirers and fellow comedians such as Jerry Lewis (who paid a brilliant homage to Stan in *The Bellboy*, 1960) and Dick Van Dyke. He spent most of his time answering all his fan letters personally, and watching

TV, particularly the old films he had made with Ollie. 'I don't know why I watch Babe all the time,' he said. 'I guess it's because the character fascinates me so much. He really is a funny, funny fellow, isn't he?' When some of his fans presented him with a colour television on his birthday, they were surprised by Stan's saying, 'That's great, that's great. By the way, didn't you know I was colour-blind?'

In February 1965, Stan suffered a heart attack and was confined to bed. On the 23rd February, he looked up at his nurse and said, 'I'd rather be skiing than doing this.' 'Do you ski, Mr Laurel?' 'No, but I'd rather be doing

that than this.' It was his final gag. He died a few minutes later. A memorial service was held in the Church of the Hills in Hollywood at which Dick Van Dyke read 'A Prayer For Clowns'. Stan's ashes were placed in the Court of Liberty at Forest Lawn Cemetery.

The plaque reads:

STAN LAUREL

(1890–1965)

A Master of Comedy

His genius in the art of humor

brought gladness to the world he loved

Stan had lived long enough to see a renewal of interest in Laurel and Hardy movies all over the world. In 1957, the producer Robert Youngson, realising the wealth of silent film comedy, put together a seventy-eight-minute compilation called *The Golden Age of Comedy*. There were extracts from movies starring Harry Langdon, Charley Chase and Ben Turpin, but the greatest revelation for most audiences came with the sequences of car-bashing from *Two Tars*, and the gigantic pie-throwing jamboree from *The Battle of the Century*. So successful was the film, that Youngson followed it with seven more such tributes. Their titles speak for themselves. *When Comedy was King* (1960), *Days of Thrills and Laughter* (1961), *Thirty Years of Fun* (1962), *MGM's Big Parade of Laughs* (1964), *Laurel and Hardy's Laughing Twenties* (1965), *The Further Perils of Laurel and Hardy* (1967) and *The Four Clowns* (1970), the clowns being Buster Keaton, Charley Chase, and Stan and Ollie. In addition to Youngson's skilful compilations, there was Jay Ward's *The Crazy World of*

Laurel and Hardy (1964). It seemed the public could not get enough of the incomparable duo.

There have also been Laurel and Hardy cartoons on TV, and a number of plays recreating the lives of The Thin One and The Fat One: *Mr Laurel and Mr Hardy*, *Blockheads* and *Stan and Ollie*, and, of course, the memorable scene in Frank Marcus's *The Killing of Sister George* (1964), in which the two female leads, a lesbian couple, dress up as Stan and Ollie for a fancy dress party.

It is quite possible that their popularity with young people may even be increased by Colorization, the trademark owned by the Hal Roach Studios. The process consists of using computers to add colour to the Laurel and Hardy shorts. *Way Out West, Helpmates* and *The Music Box* have already undergone the transformation. As the originals were not exactly masterpieces of the cameraman's art, no real damage has been done to them. In fact, some would argue that colour has given them an extra dimension. 'Yes, but does it make them funnier?' commented Hal Roach in 1986, when no longer with the company that bears his name.

In addition, there is a sacred institution that keeps the memory of Laurel and Hardy alive in the unlikely event that they should ever be forgotten. Not long before Stan's death, a group of Laurel and Hardy addicts formed an organization called The Sons of the Desert, named after one of their best pictures. The programme for the annual meeting of members was set down thus:

a.   Cocktails

b.   Business meeting and cocktails

c.   Dinner (with cocktails)

d.   After-dinner speeches and cocktails, in-cluding the following toasts: 1) 'To Stan' 2) 'To Babe' 3) 'To Fin' 4) 'To Mae Busch and Charlie Hall – who are eternally ever-popular.'

e.   Cocktails

f.   Coffee and cocktails

g.   Showing of Laurel and Hardy film

h.   After-film critique and cocktails

i.   After-after-film critique and cocktails

According to one of the articles of the constitution: 'Hopefully, and seriously, The Sons of the Desert, in the strong desire to perpetuate the spirit and genius of Laurel and Hardy will conduct activities ultimately and always devoted to the preservation of their films and the encouragement of their showing everywhere.'

Thankfully, the films have been preserved and are continually shown everywhere. The innocent appeal of Laurel and Hardy is as strong as ever, even in the more cynical world of the last decade of the twentieth century. What makes them perennial favourites is their contrasting appearance, the pleasure of familiarity derived from the characters' reactions to events – Ollie twiddling his thumbs and tie, Stan scratching his head and crying – but, mainly, their ability to awaken the child in us all. As Jack Benny said, 'By placing themselves into basic situations and then having some-thing go wrong, they are understood by people of all ages and walks of life . . . Jokes may become outdated, but the type of comedy Laurel and Hardy did will always live with us.'

FILMOGRAPHY

The director is indicated in brackets.

Hal Roach Productions

1917

Lucky Dog (Jess Robbins)

1927

Duck Soup (Fred L. Guiol)

Slipping Wives (Fred L. Guiol)

Love 'em and Weep (Fred L. Guiol)

Why Girls Love Sailors (Fred L. Guiol)

Hats Off (Hal Yates)

Do Detectives Think? (Fred L. Guiol)

Putting Pants on Philip (Fred L. Guiol)

The Battle of the Century (Clyde A. Bruckman)

1928

Leave 'Em Laughing (Clyde A. Bruckman)

Flying Elephants (Fred Butler)

The Finishing Touch (Clyde A. Bruckman)

From Soup to Nuts (Edgar Kennedy)

You're Darn Tootin (UK The Music Blasters) (Edgar Kennedy)

Their Purple Moment (James Parrot)

Should Married Men Go Home? (James Parrott)

Early to Bed (Emmett Flynn)

Two Tars (James Parrott)

Habeas Corpus (Leo McCarey)

We Faw Down (Leo McCarey)

1929

Liberty (Leo McCarey)

Wrong Again (Leo McCarey)

That's My Wife (Lloyd French)

Big Business (James W. Horne)

Unaccustomed As We Are (Lewis R. Foster)

Double Whoopee (Lewis R. Foster)

Berth Marks (Lewis R. Foster)

Men O' War (Lewis R. Foster)

Perfect Day (James Parrott)

They Go Boom (James Parrott)

Bacon Grabbers (Lewis R. Foster)

The Hoose-Gow (James Parrott)

The Hollywood Revue of 1929 (Charles F. Reisner)

Angora Love (Lewis R. Foster)

1930

Night Owls (James Parrott)

Blotto (James Parrott)

Brats (James Parrott)

Below Zero (James Parrott)

Hog Wild (James Parrott)

The Laurel and Hardy Murder Case (James Parrott)

Another Fine Mess (James Parrott)

1931

Be Big (James Parrott)

Chickens Come Home (James W. Horne)

The Stolen Jools (UK The Slippery Pearls) (William McGann)

Laughing Gravy (James W. Horne)

Our Wife (James W. Horne)

Pardon Us (James Parrott)

Come Clean (James W. Horne)

One Good Turn (James W. Horne)

Beau Hunks (UK Beau Chumps) (James W. Horne)

On the Loose (Hal Roach)

1932

Helpmates (James Parrott)

Any Old Port (James W. Horne)

The Music Box (James Parrott)

The Chimp (James Parrott)

County Hospital (James Parrott)

'Scram!' (Raymond McCarey)

Pack up your Troubles (George Marshall)

Their First Mistake (George Marshall)

Towed in a Hole (George Marshall)

1933

Twice Two (James Parrott)

Me and My Pal (Charles Rogers, Lloyd French)

Fra Diavolo (Hal Roach, Charles Rogers)

The Midnight Patrol (Lloyd French)

Busy Bodies (Lloyd French)

Wild Roses (Robert F. McGowan)

Dirty Work (Lloyd French)

Sons of the Desert (UK Fraternally Yours) (William A. Seiter)

1934

Oliver the Eighth (Lloyd French)

Hollywood Party (Richard Boleslawski)

Going Bye-Bye! (Charles Rogers)

Them Thar Hills (Charles Rogers)

Babes in Toyland (Charles Rogers)

The Live Ghost (Charles Rogers)

1935

Tit for Tat (Charles Rogers)

The Fixer-Uppers (Charles Rogers)

Thicker than Water (James W. Horne)

Bonnie Scotland (James W. Horne)

1936

The Bohemian Girl (James W. Horne, Charles Rogers)

On the Wrong Trek (Charles Parrott)

Our Relations (Harry Lachman)

1937

Way Out West (James W. Horne)

Pick a Star (Edward Sedgwick)

1938

Swiss Miss (John G. Blystone)

Block-Heads (John G. Blystone)

1939

The Flying Deuces (Boris Morros)

Zenobia (UK Elephants Never Forget) (Gordon Douglas) Hardy only

1940

A Chump at Oxford (Alfred Goulding)

Saps at Sea (Gordon Douglas)

Twentieth Century-Fox

1941

Great Guns (Monty Banks)

1942

A-Haunting We Will Go (Alfred Werker)

1943

The Tree in a Test Tube (Charles MacDonald)

Metro Goldwyn Meyer

1900

Air Raid Wardens (Edward Sedgwick)

Twentieth Century-Fox

1900

Jitterbugs (Malcolm St Clair)

The Dancing Masters (Malcolm St Clair)

1944

The Big Noise (Malcolm St Clair)

1945

The Bullfighters (Malcolm St Clair)

Metro Goldwyn Mayer

1900

Nothing But Trouble (Sam Taylor)

Republic

1949

The Fighting Kentuckian (George Waggner)
Hardy only

1950

Riding High (Frank Capra)
Hardy only

Les Films Sirius, Franco-London Films, Fortezza Films

1951

Atoll K (Leo Joannon)

Index

A Chump at Oxford (1940); *35*, 98, *98*, *99*
A-Haunting We Will Go (1942); *100*, *101*, 101
Adrian, Iris; 87
Agee, James; 92
Air Raid Wardens (1943); 102, *103*
Anderson, Gilbert M.; 20
Angora Love (1929); *61*, 61
Another Fine Mess (1930); 72
Arbuckle, Fatty; 47
Ardell, Alyce; 85
Atoll K (1951); *112*, 113

Babes in Toyland (1934); 83, *84*
Bacon Grabbers (1929); 61
Balfe, Michael; 87
Banks, Monty; 101
Barrymore, Lionel; 72
Battle of the Century, The (1927); *47*, 47, *48–49*
Be Big (1931); *10*, *43*, 72, *73*
Beau Hunks (UK: 'Beau Chumps') (1931); *79*, 79
Beery, Wallace; 78
Below Zero (1930); *62*, 72, *72*, *120*
Benny, Jack; 123
Berth Marks (1929); 66, *67*
Big Business (1929); *43*, 56
Big House, The; 78
Big Noise, The (1944); 102, *104–5*
Blaine, Vivian; *59*, 102
Block-Heads (1938); *9*, *92*, *93*, 93
Bohemian Girl, The (1936); *86*, 87
Bonnie Scotland (1935); *39*, *85*, 85
Brady, Alice; 97
Brats (1930); 33, 69, *70*, *71*
Brownlee, Frank; 81
Bruckman, Clyde A.; 39, 47
Bullfighters, The (1945); *106*, 107
Buñel, Luis; 56
Burke, Billie; 97
Busch, Mae; 42, *42*, 64, 68, 82, *82*, 86, 123
Busy Bodies (1933); *41*

Call of the Cuckoos (1927); *44*
Capra, Frank; 111
Chaplin, Charlie; 8, 15, 17, *17*, 19, 20, 61, *110*, 110
Chase, Charley; *44*, 82, *83*, 121
Chickens Come Home (1931); *42*
Chien Andalou, Un 56
Conklin, Chester; 20
Cooke, Baldwin; 20
Cramer, Dick; 99
Crazy World of Laurel and Hardy, The (1964); 121
Crosby, Bing; 39, 111
Cushing, Peter; 98

Dahlberg, Mae Charlotte; 20, 33, 97

Dali, Salvador; 56
Dancing Masters, The (1943); *102*, 102
Dandoe, Arthur; 19
Days of Thrills and Laughter (1961); 121
Dearing, Eddie; 107
Delair, Suzy; 113
Double Whoopee (1929); *60*, 60
Duck Soup (1933); 39
Dumont, Margaret; 102

Early to Bed (1928); *36*
Edwards, Ralph; 113
Enough To Do (1926); 33
Essanay Film Company; 21

Fetchit, Stepin; 97
Fighting Kentuckian, The (1949); *111*, 111
Finishing Touch, The (1928); *51*, 51
Finlayson, James; *11*, 42, *43*, 44, 56, *69*, 72, 78, 81, 86, 87, 89, 99, 123
Fixer Uppers, The (1935); 84
Flying Deuces, The (1939); 97
Ford, Model T; 66
Foster, Lewis R.; 64, *69*
Four Clowns, The (1970); 121
Fra Diavolo (1933); 81, 87
From Soup to Nuts (1928); *52*, 53
Further Perils of Laurel and Hardy, The (1967); 121

Garvin, Anita; *10*, 42, *43*, 53
Get 'Em Young (1926); 33
Gilbert, Billy; 74
Going My Way (1944); 39
Golden Age of Comedy, The (1957); 121
Great Guns (1941); *40*, 101
Grierson, John; 10
Guiol, Fred L.; 47

Hale, Alan; 87
Hall, Charlie; *11*, *29*, 42, 51, 74, 123
Hamilton, Alice; 20
Hardy, Lucille (née Jones); 97, 109, *110*, 118
Hardy, Myrtle Lee (née Reeves); 33, 56, 85, 97
Harlow, Jean; *60*, 60–61, 79
Hatley, T. Marvin; 64
Hats Off (1927); 44, 72
Helpmates (1932); 73, *74*
Hog Wild (1930); *10*, 69
Horne, James W.; 79
Hurley, Edgar; 20
Hurley, Wren; 20

Jazz Singer, The (1927); 61
Jefferson Theatre Group; 15
Jefferson, Arthur J.; 15

Jitterbugs (1943); *58–9*, 102, *103*
Joannon, Leo; 113

Kalem Studios; 20
Karno, Fred; 15, 19, 110
Keaton, Buster; 64, 121
Keith, Isabelle; *10*, 43
Kennedy, Edgar; 42, 51, *51*, 53, 56, 61, 64, 66, 102
Kerr, Walter; 38
Keystone Studios; 20
King, Dennis; 81

Laemmle, Carl; 20
Langdon, Harry; 8, 20, 64, *96*, 97, 98, 121
Laughing Gravy (1931); *28*, *123*
Laurel, Ida Kitaeva (née Raphael); 10, *107*, 109, *110*, 118
Laurel, Lois (née Neilson); 33, 37, 84
Laurel, Lois (daughter); 57, *57*, *89*, 89
Laurel, Vera Ivanova (née Shuvalova); 97, 100
Laurel, Virginia Ruth (née Rogers); 85, 97, 100
Laurel and Hardy Murder Case, The (1930); 72, *73*
Laurel and Hardy Revue, The (Stage); 100
Laurel and Hardy's Laughing Twenties (1965); 121
Leave 'Em Laughing (1928); *50*, 51
Leo, Ted; 19
Lewis, Jerry; 118
Liberty (1929); *94*
Lloyd, Harold; 8, 33, 64
Long, Walter; 78
Love 'Em and Weep (1927); 42
Lubin Motion Picture Company; 26
Lucky Dog, The (1917); *21*, 21, 27

MacDonald, Edward; 101
Marceau, Marcel; 15
Marx Brothers, The; 39
McCabe, John; 15, 47, 118
McCarey, Leo; 39, 47, 53, 69
McDaniel, Hattie; 97
Men O' War (1929); 68, *69*
Metcalfe, Madge; 15
MGM Studios; 69, 81, 102
MGM's Big Parade of Laughs (1964); 121
Miller, Henry; 51
Mitchum, Robert; 102
Morris, Chester; 78
Morse, Viola; 56, 97
Mud and Sand (1922); *31*, 33
Music Box, The (1932); 44, 73–4, *75*

Noise From the Deep, A(1913); 47
Normand, Mabel; *19*, 20, 47

North British Animated Picture Co.; 15
Nothing But Trouble (1945); 107
Nuts in May (1917); 20

Our Relations (1936); *87*, 87

Pack up your Troubles (1932); *80*, 81, 121
Paper-Hanger's Helper, The (1915); 27
Pardon Us (UK: *Jailbirds*) (1931); 76, 78, *78*
Parrott, James; 47
Perfect Clown, The (1926); 27
Perfect Day, The (1929); *66*, 66
Pick a Star (1937); 89
Playmates (1918); 33
Power, Tyrone; 107
Putting Pants on Philip (1927); *7*, 38, *38*, 42

Ralston, Vera; 111
Ramish, Adolph; 20
Ray, Bobby; 27
Reed, Jim; 19
Republic Pictures; 111
Riding High (1950); 111
RKO Pictures; 97
Roach, Hal Jr.; *114*, 115
Roach, Hal; 33, *46*, 61, 69, 78, 81, 93, 100, *114*, 121
Rogers, Charley; 81
Rogue Song, The (1930); 72

Sailors Beware (1927); 34
Saps at Sea (1940); *9*, 98, *99*
Second Hundred Years, The (1927); 42, *45*
Semon, Larry; *27*, 33
Sennett, Mack; 20, 33
Sons of the Desert (1933); *58*, 64, *82*, 82, *122*
Sons of the Desert, The; 121, 123
St. Clair, Malcolm; 107
Stevens, George; 39
Sugar Daddies (1927); *11*
Swiss Miss (1938); *11*, 89

Taylor, Robert; 98
Taylor, Sam; 107
That's My Wife (1929); *58*, 59
The Wizard of Oz (1925); 33
Their First Mistake (1932); *68*, 68
Their Purple Moment (1928); 57
Thirty Years of Fun (1962); 121
This Is Your Life (NBC); 113
Tibbett, Lawrence; 72
Todd, Thelma; 64, *71*, 81, 86, 87
Tosi, Luigi; 113
Turpin, Ben; *99*, 121
Twentieth Century Fox; 101
Two Tars (1928); *56*, 56

Unaccustomed As We Are (1929); 64

Universal Studios; 20

Van Dyke, Dick; 118, 120
Vitagraph; 33

Way Out West (1936); 64, 88, *88, 89, 90–91*

Wayne, John; 111, *111*
We Faw Down (1928); 57
Wee Georgie Wood; 15
West, Billy; 30

When Comedy Was King (1960); 121
Williamson, Robbin; 20
Wright, Basil; 69
Wrong Again (1928); 56

Yank at Oxford, A (MGM); 98

Yes, Yes, Nanette! (1925); 33
You're Darn Tootin' (1928); 53, *53, 54–55*
Youngson, Robert; 121

Zenobia (1939; *96, 97, 97*